The Ashley Dancers

∞

A Novel

By Roland Verfaillie

Copyright © 2012 Purple Onion Press
All rights reserved
Published by Purple Onion Press
San Francisco, CA
Toronto, Canada

Designed and produced by Sigmund Rich, Purple Onion Press

Other works by Roland Verfaillie published
by Purple Onion Press:
The Lie (screenplay)
The book of job(s)
The second book of job(s)
Hill of Sorrow/Mountain of Joy (Collected Poems)
Waking Up In Dreams (Collected Poems)
L'heure Bleue (Collected Poems)

No part of this book may be reproduced, stored in any retrieval system, or transmitted in any form, by any means, including mechanical, electronic, recording, or otherwise, without written permission of the publisher.

Writers Guild of America, East, Inc.
Registration Number: 129052

The Ashley Dancers
ISBN 978-0-9787085-6-6

Preface

Not your ordinary bar...

This book is about a bar. A bar which is now legendary. It is no longer there; having been bought by a restaurant chain several years ago. I can tell you, though, it hasn't been forgotten. There are certain places that we will always remember, though our recollections of what they were actually like have been modified. Bearing witness to the past is a riddle to be solved; its solution based upon an assortment of loose facts embellished by our imaginations. A memory is an attempt to recollect something forgotten. The act of remembering, in this instance, is like distilling whiskey. We may drink to remember or to forget, or to add luster to a dull day. However euphorically we recall the past, it was only simple mash to begin with. The reveries of a whiskey high, like a fine-tuned memory, trump its humble origin. The Ashley is like that for me. Over time, I must admit, it's more like a hang-over than a lasting high.

Most memorable was the dancing. People with virtually no rhythm swarmed to the Ashley in disproportionately large numbers. They came to dance to some good bands. So it goes to say that it wasn't the bands' fault. I suspect that the bad dancers drove the good dancers away. Or, as I have speculated, good dancers became bad dancers in the cuisinart-blades of the Ashley's dance floor.

So what makes me a dance critic? In particular, what right do I have to criticize people who are, after all, just out to enjoy themselves? So what if they're not dance virtuosos. And to be honest, I can't dance worth a damn. I would not be invited to sit with the panel of judges on *Dancing with the Stars*. However, this book is more than a story about a legendary, Florida bar, or about of people who can't dance. It is the latter observation which defines the legend of the Ashley – one that is rooted deeply in its history.

Dance…

Dance is one of the earliest forms of communication. It encompasses the emerging culture's history, its rituals and its customs. In short, its cosmology. Its lexicon is expressed in movement and gesture and set to rhythm and tempo that has a correlation to the paragraph, chapter and verse of written composition. Each dance movement might symbolize a noun or a verb. Simply put; think of dance movement as an action-based vocabulary for story-telling. This explanation is tied to the history and origins of dance. Exactly when dance was first introduced cannot be ascertained for certain. The earliest, tangible record of dance was discovered in wall-paintings in the Rock Shelters of Bhimbetka in India. Paintings dating back nine-thousand years. Today, not all dances are about story-telling. The evolution of dance has produced many permutations; ranging from mating and healing to dances that are codified according to their technique and a professional dancer's proficiency. Dance as recreation, sport and entertainment are the ones with which we are most familiar. The dancing performed at the Ashley, is dance most normal people have never…ever before experienced. Without the phenomenally weird dancing that they did; the Ashley would be just another charming, small town bar. You see, the place and the people are inextricably connected. In unison they are legendary. The dancers, who plied their skills on the dance floor, were as refined and graceful as a horse-drawn plow turning over rocky soil in preparation for planting. What might grow from what they started? Well, only time will tell. You would be gravely mistaken if you take what I say to be a gross exaggeration. And although I have dodged the many persistent attempts to get me to dance, I know the error of my resistance. And this is the segway to answering why I chose the Ashley and the Millennium Dance Contest to tell its story.

This story is about those who can dance and those who can't. It is about the chaos which ensues when the balance is tipped over in favor of those who can't. And the forces which arise when there is no rational mediator to help restore the balance. When either political parties or nature's seasons are in conflict and unable to reach consensus, then a third party will invariably arise to re-establish order.

And like global warming, riots and full scale revolutions, there comes shock and discomfiture. There is also uncertainty, and a whole new set of anxieties, in anticipation of the kinds of change something born of conflict will bring. For what may arrive, with equal possibility, will be either the four-horsemen of the Apocalypse or the phoenix reassembling from the ashes. I prefer the fire and the phoenix because it resonates with our myth-ruled imaginations - and supports the persistence of hope; the non-rational belief upon which we all too naively depend. Still, reconstruction is born of destruction. The Ashley's Millennium Dance Contest accompanied by a late-season hurricane represents the forces through which nature – and a mean attempt at social engineering - sought to restore the balance.

The Dance of the Stoat

Ends with the Death of the Rabbit

The Ashley
Stuart, Florida

This isn't some ordinary drinking place. No dreary whiskey bar of the last-resort. This is a neighborhood bar called the Ashley. Where the social life begins after the indigo shades of a mid-summer's sunset fade to black. And the first sounds you notice come from the sizzle of the neon sign shorting in a gentle rain. Like all things local, it's *kinky* - a term denoting pride among Stuart's residents. Unlike its competitors along Osceola Street, it's a local hang-out. It's located at the town center where strollers outnumber the through- traffic on the one-way street. I frequent the place because my wife likes to dance. I don't much enjoy the past time, but the atmosphere's...well interesting. Moreover, it's outright entertaining. The entertainment is the spectacle created by those who migrate to the twenty-square-foot dance floor and attempt to bring their fits of herky-jerky gyrations into synch with the beat of a live band. My trips to the Ashley became a week-end ritual; and I might go so far as to say a kind of penitential Bardo state. That is, in the manner of the pre-requisite torment theoretically endured by recently deceased Hindus before they can pass on to a higher plane of existence. My Bardo, is likewise preparing me for a higher plane. In my case, to become a decent dance partner. It is also a marriage breaker, because my wife, Eve, is a dance addict. And like all the other kinds of addicts, dancers are a subculture of obsessed and compulsive creatures. Once the music begins, they become slavering movers and shakers; junkies to the rhythms that invariably control them. They just can't help themselves. And there isn't an effective intervention that will stop them. Like the alcoholic who prefers the company of a drinking partner, Eve desires a dance partner.

Eve's dancing has morally degraded her. She will dance with anyone. Indiscriminately, choosing a partner of either gender, or engaging in a shameless conjugation of writhing flesh which pushes the limits of orgasmic ecstasy. Call me possessive, but I want exclusive rights to Eve's climactic episodes. Maybe I exaggerate, but not all that much. Or perhaps I'm just jealous of those who are born with natural rhythm. Or, I'm homophobic; erroneously assuming that Latin men who wiggle are gay. I use the Latin male as an example because Eve gets mesmerized by the Hispanic guy who slithers to the beat of the Cha-Cha like a frenzied cobra. I can't snap her out of her trance when she is fixated on the gyrating pelvis of a dancing lothario dressed like Zorro.

My handicap is having been born a pale, white guy with genetic disadvantages. I have a mixed ancestral heritage of French and Irish. People who danced the minuet and performed stepdance without moving their upper torsos. This produced in me the genetic propensity to dance with the grace of an industrial jack hammer. Nevertheless, I'm determined to try and do better. With the right partner who knows. With enough practice, a man ungifted in the art of dance may pass for average. I'd settle for that. Just to be able to dance well enough to spare both of us serious embarrassment. I found that I could practice among my kindred dance challenged at the Ashley; where even I might pass for a contestant in the senior division of "Dancing with the Stars."

So, there it is. I'm trying to win Eve over by bettering myself as a man – who can dance. Because, Eve will leave me for another man who's mating dance is more seductive than mine. Dance is no mere hobby engaged in solely by people with ADD or with meth habits. Students of ancient history will tell you, that dance has been around for thousands of years. It isn't just a hyperactive display of rhythmic agility, or an exhibition of grace and dexterity. It was frequently used by some suitor or other to show feelings for one of the other gender. It is linked to the origin of, "love making." Now it is far less pretentious. It *is* love making, and it isn't limited to the "other gender." Most club-dancing is borderline pornographic, where *Dirty Dancing* and asking a complete stranger to dance is synonymous. I am determined to be a competitor. No, a winner. Even if I have to carry a concealed weapon on the dance floor.

The Ashley plays an important role in this pursuit. It is basic training. And like the Marine Corps' Paris Island, the Ashley is fraught with significant physical risk to the uninitiated. You've seen the dance shows where young dancers defy gravity and bend into contortions as spectacular as the feats performed by Cirque du Sole. Even those shows which select celebrity klutzes with visible handicaps learn to dance like professionals in the hands of a competent master. I had figured out after a season or two that the dance instructor is sexual bait that will make a Frankenstein wearing ski boots plié like Baryshnikov about to burst his cuckold. Each season the E News invariably exposes at least one dance couple whose been rehearsing horizontally off studio. How can this *not* happen? Dance promises equal measures of pain and pleasure. Any man or woman would Hip Hop naked through a forest of bramble bushes engulfed in flames if following the lead of Svetlana or Sven. Although eve doesn't arrive at the Ashley in seven coats of spray-on tan and silicone breast implants, she is every bit as attractive. If I have to dance I'd just as soon have her as my partner. Besides I need some points to win her over. She's all but had it with me. And not just because I can't dance. She has had years to grind her axe against all of my alleged offenses – which I'd rather not go into right now. But suffice it to say, she is ready to divorce me unless I offer some payback. And dancing with her might prevent her from filing for divorce.

So here it is. My debut with "So You Think You Can Dance," at the Ashley. A bar with the chutzpah to sponsor its own dance competition fashioned after the TV show. At this place the answer to the challenge, "So You Think You Can Dance," is, Well… You Can't. Some of those on the syndicated TV show know they can't either, but it doesn't stop them from making fools of themselves. If they can – make fools of themselves – then, so can I. There's a lot more at stake here than simply looking foolish.

CHAPTER 1

Eve was born in Florida. She thinks that she is as native to Florida as the Mayflower settlers were to Plymouth, Massachusetts. I don't argue the difference because to do so would be futile; requiring us to re-write the history books and base each chapter on red neck folk lore, and White Supremist doctrine. Eve's parents hail from Everglades City, their idea of the Garden of Eden. They are even more stubborn than Eve in their claim to being founding fathers; ignoring the fact that Colusa Indians had established flourishing settlements there a few millennia before their spontaneous arrival. Eve's clan-folk despise the Northern carpetbaggers who they say have spoiled the pristine paradise of their Creation myth. I am tolerated, although a Yankee, because I am deemed worthy by Jimmie, Eve's father, because I like NASCAR, and I don't, ' act, 'all uppity like a lot of Northerners do.' Besides, Evelyn, Eve's mother, thinks I look like Jim Foxworthy. So, from her perspective, 'I could pass.' The rest of the Northern migrants are summarily disregarded and considered outsiders to their antebellum caste system. I avoid any conversations that might re-ignite the still smoldering hostilities of the Civil War. Like dance, I will tolerate the mild insults to my person. I don't share their illusion that there is an established culture here. The fact that the land mass of Florida resembles an appendix goes beyond analogy. The majority of indigestible, un-assimilative types from the North East and Mid-Atlantic states have steadily settled in Florida. They end up nesting in crowded rookeries along both the Gulf and Atlantic coastlines.

I've digressed. But the short anthropology of South Florida is important to understanding the extraordinary diversity of the locals – meaning people originally from somewhere else – both in dialect and dance. The New Jersey and Maryland gum-smacking slang-slingers, New York nasal enunciators and Mason-Dixon diphthong danglers grate on one another's auditory sensibilities in a relentless dual of discordant dialects. Speech alone creates a Tower of Babble making what should pass for social politesse a lexicon battleground. Add to this confusion, the regional dance variations of this non-homogenous population and you have chaos turned loose upon the dance floor. The Ashley is ground-zero for what catastrophic damage such a melting pot of implosive forces might produce.

The Ashley was built in 1900. It was Stuart's first bank and was aptly named...the Stuart Bank. It was in 1915 that a few of Stuart's ill-bred ancestors set the stage, so to speak, for the Ashley's modern legacy. The ancestors in this situation were a gang of outlaws. Leave it to the modern day romantics to glorify the American anti-hero, and name a bar after the n'er do wells. The culprits were the Ashley brothers, John and Bob. They formed the gang that robbed the Stuart Bank in 1915. The gang, comprised of John and Bob Ashley along with Kid Lowe, actually botched the job. Their take that afternoon was... Well, disappointing. Kid Lowe, angry with John over the puny take, shot John Ashley right there on the spot. The bullet shattered John's jaw, and came to rest against his right eye. The wound resulted in the loss of the eye, the later implantation of a teddy bear, glass-eye prosthetic and a black eye patch. The visage of a pirate, a Prussian duelist, a war hero? No. Just one ugly, pissed-off mother fucker hiding all that humiliation behind a silk eye-patch, an expensive Brookes Brothers suit and a new Thompson sub-machine gun.

Well, picture that: Poor John, shot point blank, hopping about in a cloud of black powder, no doubt deafened by the blast of the pistol, doing the Jig. Now, keeping that picture in mind, close your eyes (hopefully both of them), and let yourself be guided (trust me) to the edge of the dance floor of the Ashley. Now, open your eyes. What do you see? By God, John Ashley lives again...and the beat goes on.

_____ CHAPTER 2_____

"Anyone can fake it, but aren't you tired of fumbling across the dance floor, stepping on toes in front of your friends and family? For those of you who have always admired fine dancers from afar but have never found the time to pursue the skill yourselves,...now is your chance."

From, "Shall We Dance?"
by, Manine Rosa Golden

This story is about dance, as everything so far leading up to this point suggests. It is also a story about using dance as it had always been intended – to attract a mate. These two elements are inextricably related. I will give fair consideration to other interpretations of the origin of dance. But because I'm no scholar of the humanities, I'll have to supply references, anecdotes, and scads of erudite hypotheses that (I'll admit now), I've made up. I am nevertheless as eminently qualified as any academic in the field of dance. That I can't dance worth a shit doesn't disqualify me as long as I don't pretend to be a dance coach. I know my limits. It was only fairly recently that dance became the province of academic scholars. It wasn't even recognized as an academic discipline until the early 1920s. It wasn't until later in the century that dance research based on the observation of its performance across cultures culminated in a bone fide curriculum of college course work. I can only imagine my father's reaction to his son declaring a major in *Dance*. My major in Psychology was hard enough for him to accept. This is nothing compared to the worries he'd have expressed if I were to have declared myself a dance major. I can only say that it will take a better psychologist than myself to understand my fear of dancing; a fear whose explanation lies much deeper than being uncoordinated. I remember when psychotherapy co-opted with dance to help expand the human potential. Gestalt therapists were keen on trying to coerce me to dance and sing in order to free me from the constraints of my rigid personality. I would have gladly submitted to electroshock therapy or a week in an isolation tank than perform a song and dance routine before a group of Gestaltists. I was excommunicated from the Gestalt community as the result of my obstinacy. I realize now that overcoming my 'blocks' to genuineness and wholeness might have made things easier for me later. It is not badge of honor to carry one's rigidity to the dance floor. I now know that there are soft characteristics in men that turn some women on. Crying and dancing are two of them. I was a miserable failure at both. I became determined to excel in one or both. It was beyond my imagining as to which of these skills it would be. The outcome shall remain a mystery for now. To divulge the ending now, although expeditious and straight to the point, would spoil the ending for you. Besides there are greater forces at work than those governing the organic laws of attraction. Intra-species competition for a mate is brutal, and this brutality cannot be tamed by society's codes or governmental laws. When brought into the area of competition it is a no holds barred Octagon sport. This one, of course, being squared off as a dance floor. Posts, ropes and padding shouldn't be omitted.

Dance as the central theme is very appropriate because dance is the primordial social organizing force, the progenitor of culture itself. Many cultures are even defined by dance. Dance is universal. It is the language of rhythmic and patterned bodily movements that has permutated into hundreds of regional customs and diverse forms. It is assumedly easily learned by almost everyone in the indigenous culture, except the uncoordinated. It shames me to see the blind and the deaf dance better than I. I'm not stooping low when I say that persons confined to wheel chairs and rolled onto the dance floor can move more fluidly than I.

    What amazed me as Eve and I took a table near the dance floor, and watched people pair up, and step to the dance floor was that no one could dance. It was a band night. The Vagrants were performing. They're a versatile band that can play any number from the seventies to contemporary mainstream. Their instrumental and vocal rendition of the artists' music is like listening to the original group performing live on stage. The point I'm making here, is that it wasn't the band's fault that no one could dance. The band was musically correct. The dancers, every one of them, seemed to be afflicted with Saint Vitus Dance, maybe 'myospastic arrhythmia,' to coin a disease. People full of erumpent energies were letting themselves go this way and that like a swarm of angry hornets suddenly shaken from their nest by a playful pit bull. So when Eve leaned over to shout into my ear, "Stewart, aren't you going to ask me to dance?" I was shocked. Shocked that she would voluntarily enter the fray and have me lead the way. To me it would have invited the same risk as idling at the on ramp to I-95 at rush hour in my Volkswagen Beetle, and flooring the gas pedal in an attempt to squeeze between two semis doing eighty miles an hour. I didn't share these terrifying thoughts with her. I truly thought she was testing me; waiting for me to say something valiant like: 'Into the maelstrom we shall not go, lest death and destruction follow'. I said the next best thing I could think of. I simply shouted back: "How 'bout waiting for them to play an eighties number?", and to the waitress: "Please, another Corona and a Cabernet... no, instead make mine a vodka-on-the-rocks...a double."

"Each couple is made up of a leader and a follower. The leader decides the figures to dance and their order. The follower, normally unaware of which figure the leader will choose, must be able to follow based on the leader's suggestions. The leader leads through the distribution of weight. For example, in order to step forward with the right foot, weight must be settled on the left foot. The follower must respond to this distribution of weight, inferring what the next step will be. As a leader, it is important to communicate the dance plan clearly and confidently. As a follower, it is important not to resist."

From, "Shall We dance,"
By, Manine Rosa Golden

As luck, and the end of Eve's patience would have it, we left before the band got to 1978. The Ashley dancers were doing what looked like the disco-Macarena when we left. Don't construe from my remarks that I'm a dance snob with an Astaire-Rogers more-graceful-than-thou attitude. In fairness to myself, I'm actually a slightly, below average dancer who can be ratcheted up to average with the right partner. Eve can dance. She is far above average on the dance floor, and her range is from Latin to line. She can even jitter-bug, go under the legs and over-the-shoulder of her partner and never show her panties. But she's not the best partner for me, because *she can't not lead*, and *I won't follow*. I think it's because of a height and gait disparity, not a control-freak, male privilege thing. But this isn't the reason I didn't dance with Eve that night. I've danced with her plenty over the years we've been together. On the occasion I mentioned, It had everything to do with being out-numbered. Out-numbered by people who just couldn't dance if their lives depended on it. The below average dancers like me didn't stand a chance of being bumped up to average. Conspicuously missing were the Eves; the men and women of poise, grace and acrobatic agility. Lacking entirely, were those with the ability to lead the two-left-feet-encumbered through the trials of a two-step. How was it possible?, I asked myself, that so many people who can't dance could end up at the same place, at the same time . Carried as it were on strong eddies far from the social mainstream, only to find themselves beached and gasping for air far from their natural element. I speculated that this one night was a fluke. And that Eve and I had accidentally stumbled onto a movie set, and got swept up in a scene before hidden cameras filming an indoor take of Running *with the Bulls*. I assured myself that it was a phenomenon not likely to repeat itself. Was I wrong.

CHAPTER 3

"When you go dancing in public, you may notice that other couples dance the same dance differently. There are many schools of dance, and each has a unique approach to the individual dances...If you see a couple dancing the foxtrot differently than you, and if you like their approach better, ask them about it."

From, "Shall We Dance?"
by, Manine Rosa Golden

Ask them about it indeed! This is the kind of question a lunatic would ask an Ashley dancer. Such a lunatic would say, " Gee, my cousin who fell off his third floor condominium balcony last year, does the...a...rumba sort'a like you do. Where did you learn to do it so...freestyle, so... interestingly inventive?" A question to which the Ashley dancer would no doubt reply, "It's something I just learned tonight. See the dots on the floor. I just move with them. I just *connect* with each one of them. It's a force I can't explain." The dots, of course, are produced by the reflections of the revolving mirrored ball suspended from the ceiling. A chiaroscuro of infinitesimal little beacons tracing the four corners of the bar. It should have served as a warning to the bobbing and weaving dancers adrift in dangerous cross-currents of the collision course on which every couple was headed.

Yes, I did go back to the Ashley...again, and again. And I still do. I even take along friends of mine who had never patronized the establishment. Many hypnotically shuffle to the dance floor with partner in tow only to exhibit their own inevitable failures as if they were infected by some mysterious limb paralyzing pathogen. The only other experience like this one that I'd ever before encountered was the result of drinking the punch at an acid party. When the entire evening involved doing slow motion skeleton and teddy-bear line dances to the tunes of the Grateful Dead.

I feel a little guilty being so critical of the Ashley dancers. It is the kind of guilt you feel when you laugh at the guy who just wiped out the corner hot dog stand before you realize his Seeing Eye dog just chased a stray cat. I want this to read as a self-help guide. Like another, "[Something] For Idiots" book. Better still, an infomercial blockbuster that millions of discouraged and rejected males will tune into, buy the book and the DVD set, and go on to become successful dancers and lovers. I feel passionately about reforming the disenfranchised party-goers who won't dance while their dates get all pissy and deny them sexual favors for the rest of the week. Even the dance aficionada may benefit from a tune up. If I contribute nothing else to the world let it be this: That I might inspire real men to dance with dignity; to help move them beyond the uncoordinated epicenter of our gender - and do so without prancing or employing unnatural hip and shoulder movements. Why then, single out the Ashley and its patrons for this seemingly impossible task? Well, as experiments go, I could have made it easy and offered money to volunteers. First of all I don't have a research grant. Secondly, I like to cut to the chase and not waste time on tedious experimental trials and having to crunch a pile of statistical data. This is a group who requires nothing short of a miracle to help them. I believe in picking a difficult population, because if you can convert savages like these you can sell the idea to anyone. Without a culture of normal hominids who can dance, the rest of us will forever teeter on the brink of extinction. And most importantly, no fecund female will want to mate with us.

I figured out why Eve had insisted on the Ashley for our trysts. It was because she didn't want any competition from the other women in estrus. It was down to the finalists as far as she was concerned. She knew if she could bring me along as a husband-in-training, and succeed in teaching me to dance (the way the Patet Lau conducted social re-education), then we would both be winners. I can appreciate her motives even if they are driven by her insecurities - and an appetite for revenge. I still sought an explanation as to why the Ashley seemed to attract so many who couldn't dance. No, not so many, but all. Even ruling out that the locals may have passed on a dominant gene for hip dysplasia, there were enough tourists to have produced the occasional seasoned dancer. I'm not a native to Florida. My parents could dance. I used to watch them dust the dance floor at every occasion for celebration. My mother sang and danced like a virtuoso. I should have had a fighting chance, at least - of being an okay dancer.

I theorized all manner of anomalies – geophysical, genetic, and psychic – that might explain the problem of mass rhythm paralysis. I'm speculating that one or more of them might provide the answer. The theory at the top of my list is a geophysical hypothesis. For instance, some break in the electromagnetic grid deep below the Ashley's foundations. Some energy flux that might interfere with the fine hairs of the inner ear responsible for balance. Or maybe the opposite. Like an energy vortex stronger than the ones in Sedona. Ancient civilizations built temples and cities on these energy centers; attracted to them by some sentient powers beyond their immediate senses. This may explain why the city of Stuart constructed Confusion Corner in the town center.

Confusion Corner is the unofficial reference to the traffic round-about located in the heart of downtown Stuart. It is a name well deserved because drivers approaching the traffic circle would do as well to drive blindfolded, propelled only by a raw white-knuckled courage than to rely upon the street signs. The signs are the equivalent of waving braille semaphore flags to guide a blind man through a mine field. It is virtually the wormhole whose event horizon is Stuart's Main Street. It is indeed a chaotic dark energy force into which drivers are sucked, deprived of their sense of direction, and unceremoniously thrust into the parallel universe of the Ashley. New arrivals are easy to spot. They are easily recognized by the dazed look and tabetic shuffle they affect as they enter the bar. Lured not only by the music of the bands, but also by the pied piper of a Bachman universe whose harmony only an Ashley dancer can hear (which is similar to using a silent dog whistle to summon your pooch). Here these time travelers become hyper-attenuated organisms whose former gravitation world has lost its hold on them. They arrive in a warped fold of a parallel universe in which no one can dance.

Confusion Corner's geographical proximity to a time warping energy grid may sound like the stuff of science fiction. But, it is not. It's real. The location corresponds with the well charted energy centers mapped by researchers, Bethe Hagens and William Becker. Just check out the hexakis icosahedron grid, coordinate calculations, and point classification system they developed. I didn't make this up, although I did wildly extrapolate (guessed). So, I might off a few standard errors of measure. At the risk of waxing metaphysical, the facts support the theory to which I earlier alluded. The theory that great cities and holy places were built on sites to which their founders were drawn by subtle energies. Attracted, if you will, like iron filings to a magnet. These force fields lie below the earth's mantle, some strong, some weak. Along the strongest energy fields, people migrated in great numbers. The ancient cities these enlightened wayfarers built upon them evolved into modern cities; expanding into greater metropolises. From their power centers radiated commerce, art and culture. Look at Babylon, Luxor, Athens, Machu Picchu, Rome, New York City, and the inter-net. From city-state, to nation, to global village. Arguably, I'd opine, we've rather devolved from good to bad. I can't imagine the gods being very happy with us. Because we've really mucked things up. It was never in the grand design that we should become a global smiley face – with $ sign symbols for eyes. I can imagine the gods of creation wearing menacing frowns, and thinking up new ways to punish us. Depriving us of dance may be our curse. The greed that motivates the populace may require us to pay exorbitantly for our dance lessons. The Ashley may be the Bardo state through which we will have to earn our state of 'grace.'

We can only hope that a dance messiah will arrive along with the human cargo transported here. The One who will make the lame walk and teach the rest of us to dance. Perhaps you think I'm proposing making Hip Hop the national religion and seeing the United States become American Bandstand. True, the country could use an overhaul of its value systems. The ones on which the original commonwealth was founded. The values that were displaced over the past two-hundred by shameless greed and imperialism. Certainly this isn't a condition I or anyone else can remedy in the short term. It would amount to denying the reality of the past two-hundred years and America's meteoric rise to power. So, I will stick to the Ashley. It is small, manageable and a metaphor (if life really needs any) where a few liberal arts graduates might could make a difference. However, it may prove as difficult to bring about change there as it would the nation.

I suspect that in the home of the gods – be that heaven or Olympus – no one can dance either. In the heavenly abode there would be a conspicuous absence of *Pride,* along with ballast needed to hold an etheric body to the dance floor and allow it to move it to the rhythms of the yabyum. The gods can't dance worth a punk rocker's damn. And they can't bestow a gift they don't possess in the first place. We therefore won't be taught to dance or rescued from extinction by a power from on high. It will be up to the Eves of this world to show us the way, and teach us how to dance.

CHAPTER 4

Of all the famous highways, streets, avenues, and boulevards about which we've heard - Pennsylvania Avenue, Route 66, Park Avenue, Hollywood and Vine and Main Street U.S.A. - I'd like to add another. 61 Osceola Street, the address of the Ashley Bar.

The Cotton Club is to old downtown Harlem, as the Ashley is to revitalized, old downtown Stuart...of course, if one is willing to ignore the major contrasts of era, population density, racial majority and climate. There's still a lot to compare. For starters, both are places where a hip Renaissance took place. With much of it happening in the clubs, in the parlors of the intellectual hep cats and in the bars. Something that can only be explained as a spontaneous combustion of creative energies. The creative juices of the hip bhikkus chemically reacted and produced funky, new, indigenous art forms. Special places, immune from the materialism and surrounding cultural inertia that it caused. Fun places where the new social norm took the shape of what it could imagine. Like a new life form rising clean and shiny from the mud of an ancient river bottom. Think of the Ashley as...as a quaint little restaurant-bar featured in Florida Trend magazine...

> "Ashley's is an attractive new restaurant in the revitalized area of down-town Stuart. Ringed with small hibiscus trees, its white walls and bright striped awnings grace the corner of Osceola Street, not far away from the all-too-aptly named Confusion Corner."

Florida Trend Magazine meant well...and then in walks the 'Creature from the Indian River Lagoon' with a 2/4 fade haircut, tribal tattoos, wearing his baseball cap tilted sideways, its crown shaped like an orange carp. Believe me this is not a caricature the likes of which I would ask you to *try* to imagine. No, this is a local who I could introduce you to in the streets. He is just one of the many colorful characters who patronize the businesses of down town Stuart. The Ashley is at the heart of it all and through whose doors the craziest characters enter. Much like outlaws entering a church to seek asylum from the law.

   On any day or night of the week a visit to Stuart Main Street is a treat. There has been negative criticism in recent years that the small, downtown area has become overly populated with bars and restaurants. The chief critic and self-appointed town crier, is the unpopular politico, Armand Piccolo. He's publically condemned the Stuart Main Street organization for allowing the proliferation bars and restaurants in the compact downtown; squeezing out the sundry merchants of the James Thurber Main Street varieties. The historic downtown area, all two square blocks of it, boasts of thirteen restaurants or coffee shops. Sadly missed is the Osceola Bakery, a mom and pop establishment, once responsible for seducing countless potential heart patients to their happy caloric and insulin suicides.

Not that the restaurants and bars of this art haven haven't contributed to society or to the economy. Indeed they have. The restaurants have titillated the palates of gourmand compulsive overeaters, generated record sales of fat-burning supplements, and have inspired countless masochistic exercise programs. And the bars...well the bars make people happy (a drink costs about as much as a Prozac tablet), sociable, and able to River Dance *on* the St. Lucie River. As for those who become alcoholics, well there's

Fellowship Hall on the corner, right across the street from the Ashley, where AA meetings are held almost every day of the week, and to where truckloads of coffee, cigarettes and doughnuts are delivered as often as the Serenity Prayer. So you see, the town planners have created a balanced, symbiotic system of economic and social incest, probably modeled after their ancestry.

The Ashley is downtown Stuart's shrine. It's a holy place. I reflexively lower my voice when I say its name. Like the reverential tone you use when saying your prayers. You don't develop this kind of respect by merely seeing its picture on a post card, or glimpsing it when driving by, or looking at it from across the street. You have to enter this...this zen-bar-holy-place in order to experience the radiant power emitted by its ambiance. I remember the first time I set foot in the place. I was with Eve, and we were out on the town so to speak. It was as much an expedition, as it was a night out. We moved to Stuart after having been apartment nomads for several years since we moved back home after living in Europe. We had just bought a home in Stuart, and it was one of our early forays into new territory. Eve regarded us as returning ex-patriots. She had said to me, "Stewart, you can cut the disenfranchised American Bolshevik bull shit, and settle your ass down and your family back home where we belong. And besides, you know how important it is to me that our kids get to know their grandparents. You haven't been fair," blah, blah, blah. I caved under pressure. Capitulated to her will. Acquiesced under duress. I said, like the craven coward I'd become, "Okay, sure. Why not?" My agreement filled her with bliss over being nowhere near a foreign military base. I had worked as an American apparatchik for the Department of Defense, having become a high ranking civil service bureaucrat. My importance allowed me to wear suits and ties and attend meetings twelve hours a day. I knew by returning to the states, I'd miss the European life style: the travel, the Alpine skiing, the co-ed, fabric-free saunas and being called, "Sir", at age thirty. Eve had enjoyed her halcyon days there as well. However her meteoric career course became erratic and ultimately cooled to particle ash. This was caused by me up-rooting her every time she got settled into a job. This was because I got frequently re-assignment to bases throughout Europe. She had worked and trained in areas relating to European holistic medicine, gave birth to our two children, cursed the cold weather with bi-lingual fluency, and contracted terminal, Seasonal Affective Disorder (SAD). Unfortunately, I may have lacked some small amount of compassion for her miseries. I might have been a bit too complacent. And, after all, I had the protection of my own emotional down comforter. Eve's abstemious, "no, sir" refusals to all of my subsequent amorous flirtations marked the beginning of her anti-tyranny campaign against me. I think I can remember her using that word, 'tyranny,' when I told her we had to re-locate. It was the sixth time in nine years. I thought she had over-reacted. Well, she could have worked as a torturer for the MOSAD, or a political destabilizer for the CIA. Her ruthless methods wore me down, most notably her abstemious refusals. With little recourse, other than ignoring her 'deafening' silent treatment and the possibility of a violent coup at home, I did what any decent husband and father would do. I surrendered unconditionally. I moved us all back home. Eve rejoiced at her victory. She was finally freed from involuntary exile and was living in the Promised Land of the U.S.A. So, I was once more able to sleep naked on cool sheets in the dark-of-the-eighty-five-degree-Florida-February-nights..."yes, sir."

I must confess. I was, well, more than just a little self-centered over the years we had been together. But still [and this is where if I said I was making an apology, my rationalizing would negate it], returning, 'home,' isn't what I'd call it. It was all 'foreign' to me. No job. No decent beer. And no snow. Although, things were chilly between Eve and I for a while after re-settling. I told myself I'd have to suck it up, and move on. I wasn't prepared however for the movement the likes of which I witnessed at the Ashley. Nothing could compare.

So, this isn't just a story about dance. It's about starting over. First baby steps and then the stumbling around as I try to get my feet planted firmly under me. I didn't expect it would take so long. But then evolution can't be hurried. From the simian dragging his knuckles on the ground, to the Homo sapiens walking up-right, to Stewart dancing gracefully is a long and arduous process. My evolution will continue, and it will take place at the Ashley!

As I have been saying, it is when you set foot in the Ashley that you are struck by...curious interest. Incredulousness, comes after the dancers arrive. From the outside, the Ashley's your ordinary restaurant bar. It was cosmetically improved during the town's renaissance that took place in the 70s. The original, green-and-white striped awnings are gone, and expanses of white stucco break up the monotony of the formerly, all red-brick exterior. It resembled a turn of the century hardware store or grain station before the renovation. It would have stayed that way if Annie and Hoss Dodge hadn't bought the old landmark building in 1990, and gave it a facelift and an interior make over. They keep a scrap book by the front door that shows the stages of its renovation, along with its history-in-pictures for the Florida Heritage buffs. The renovation had transformed the Ashley into an off-beat contemporary trysting place. The entrance has been widened with double doors that swing open to admit the unsteady, thus minimizing the incidence of painful hip, head, neck and shoulder injuries. A portal, you might imagine, wide enough to admit an alien landing pod. Not impossibly, one pulled into the dizzying gyre of Confusion Corner. Pods from which emerge the natives of Stuart; infantile in their mobility, groping and sucking at the teat of, ----, the mother of Dance. Or, that of its dance partner.

The Ashley is a post card perfect place. It is side walk art on a three-dimensional scale. The windows and doors display seashore motifs in aquatint art work. The work is the artistry of Hoss Dodge. Glassine, infused with rainbow colors, absorb the sunlight and magnify an underwater world imprisoned in glass. The effect is like staring into a salt water aquarium filled with exotic marine life. Above the front double doors is the address, "61 Osceola", in bold courier script. Below, figures of sensuous women etched in five foot panes of glass beckon the hesitant patron. They are nude, Venus De Milo twins. Their bare breasts peaked by perky nipples and areola the size of medallion pancakes. So as not to offend the prudes, the ladies most private parts are modestly concealed behind swirls of 2-inch wide ribbons - held in place and in perpetuity by hardened silica. They are Windexed daily to remove the greasy finger prints of art and pancake lovers.

Enter the Ashley, more restaurant by day; more bar by night. An 'OPEN' sign is a redundancy, for you are welcome here anytime. 'Welcome' is meant in the finest Southern tradition, not in the manner of the 24/7 generation of sweat shops passing for customer friendly businesses that never close. Lose the moral shackles, and leave your inhibitions behind. Leave work and forget your worries. What breaks a sweat should be your shimmy and shake, not your manual labors. Just...relax. Have fun. Enjoy the company of old friends, or make new ones. Have lunch, don't do lunch. Don't have a drink. Just drink. The ambiance is mystical; created by interplay of street light seeping through stained glass windows. It is as solemn as a church and as quiet as the box springs of a nun's bed... until the sun goes down. I asked Eve, a religion scholar of sorts; 'if by keeping regular week-ends at the Ashley would my Easter Obligation be fulfilled?' Eve, who will brook no blasphemy, replied acerbically, "Too late for you, unrepentant fool. Your lapsed status as a Catholic expired twenty years ago. On your knees." Humbly I submitted, "Yes, Ma'm," with an air of eager expectation. Well, eager expectation quickly evaporates with the humiliation of having your genuflection mistaken for the dancer's denouement. There we stood (me, having risen like the time-lapsed sprouting of a crocus) in the narthex of this solemn, holy place. Nevertheless about to become one of the enlightened bhikku.

What I noticed when I first walked through the doors of the Ashley was the floor. I assumed that it was because I had reached my all-time low in self-esteem. You would think that with all the years of having attended parochial schools and human potential workshops, I'd be more resilient. I should have noticed the angels above. I mean that literally. Angels perched on pedestals above the front door, and around the Ashley's interior walls. Not exactly the heavenly choir variety. Not sappy, 90s angel-fad Tinkerbelle. Nothing worse than those insipid spiritual buddies with the attitude of a stalker. My friend Jack, a former bible salesman from Texarkana, described them as bail bondmen for the Big Guy. There at the ready to save you from yourself when you're doing something stupid and dangerous. And when your time does come these are the ones who taxi you the happy marketplace in the sky. Alright, point made. The angels I'm talking about are cool, stoic, kick-ass manikins with wings. Not wapentake, sword-brandishing killer commando drones sent by God to annihilate Satan's spawn. The Ashley sentries are torch bearers. Light beacons placed above the shadows to help steer the Ashley patron's on their course and light the way. Jack impressed me with his explanation of their role. By the authority vested in him by King James and the Regency Publishing House, he confidently stated, "You know in Genesis it says that the role of angels is to assist, direct and deliver God's people," and in a tone that sounded a bit sinister added, "they are also believed to execute God's will toward individuals and nations." Well, by God (sincerely), that confirmed my hunch that I'd come to the right place, and I too would be watched over protectively. Moreover, I had arrived at the right place, at the right time, and was about to participate in the risky business of learning how to dance. This undertaking would take place under the watchful eyes of the angels. We would have the protection we needed to avoid serious injury both to our bodies and our sensitive egos. There was no safer place then right here at the Ashley; the heart and the soul of downtown Stuart. We were on a mission from God. I made the mistake of sharing this revelation out loud with Eve. She is quick to judge. She told me I couldn't hang out with Jack anymore, and that we ought to plan separate vacations. She suggested that I see a travel agent and book an extended holiday in Patmos. She was certain, she told me, that all expenses might be paid by a fellowship through the Vatican. She offered to arrange everything for me through a local psychiatric facility that she had heard about from a compassionate friend. I assured her that I was just playing devil's advocate to a wild theory to which some deluded person might subscribe. Someone like Jack to whose influence I assured her I was immune. I decided on a more rational, scientific approach to the question of the angels' origins and their significance. I asked Hoss where he got the angels, and to hear his answer to the question, 'Why [fucking] angels?' So, I took the direct approach, and with the insouciance of a barfly, I asked, "Were the angels hitchhiking on the highway to heaven when you picked em up?" What I got was a startled look that reminded me of how these guys reacted on TV who had just been busted in a solicitation sting. "No...No, that was my cousin and her friend from Tampa. I was giving them a ride to the bus station." I obviously caught Hoss off guard. He was probably just feeling tired and over-worked.

I gave him a second chance, "No, not them. Them (Pointing up). Where did the angels come from?" "Why, from heaven, Stewart. At least that's what some people believe." There I had it! The answer that validated Jack's and my theories. And with the surgical cruelty of Torquemada, Eve interjects, "Hoss, Stewart's curious about the angel figures that you have on the wall pedestals. Where did you get them?" " Oh (regarding me with a mocking kindness that hurt my feelings), those. I bought those two up there from Jim over at Two Streets. I made the others from molds I casted from the originals. Jim said they came from a church out of some diocese in Philadelphia. Apparently they razed an old church. Cleared the lot to build a Burger King."

    I stood there mute before Hoss and Eve. The odd man out. I had just experienced a sudden loss of faith. Angels from Philadelphia. More refugees from the Middle Atlantic States. My only consolation was my sympathy for them. Who could blame them? How could you blame the angels for dodging the wrecking ball and the Whopper, and for fleeing so unholy a sounding place: The City of Brotherly Love? Obviously a modern-day Sodom. With wings flapping to beat the band, they made their bee line to the deep South and into the salubrious climes of Florida. Finding safety, alas, in the sanctuary of a bar. Others were sure to follow. And they are still arriving in record numbers.

    So forget the angels then. And consider the decor, particularly the art work with which the proprietors of the Ashley have tastefully....well, eclectically (as in salvage yard inventory), selected to decorate. To me they are like signs in the desert. Put there by God himself to guide the thirsting prophet to the vineyards of Mad Dog 20/20. Ashley art is a lot like the cave paintings of Lascaux. Providing a pitched black gallery that depicts the pre-recorded history of a lost and extinct tribe - finally returning home from a timeless space odyssey. Home, at last, into the torch lit bar of the Ashley.

This "mystical" leitmotif, by the way, isn't my attempt to put a New Age, Unity worship spin on the Ashley's evolution. I not a fan of New Age, Unity Church non-committal, agnostic cowardice. Give me a Southern Baptist snake handler or an Atheist any day to one of those mud sucking ecumenical bottom feeders. The Ashley phenomenon is not about religion. If you consider what it means *to be religious,* you will agree. Religion comes from the Latin word, *religare,* which means to hold back, or restrain oneself. You will never, ever see an Ashley dancer restrain himself. What you will see is the antithesis of religious temperance. Witness, if you dare, the dance of the Ashley, Southern Baptist, snake bite victim.

The real Ashley chronicles are told through its art canvases. The art work displayed throughout the Ashley is the art connoisseur's descent into chaos. There are none of the constraints generally considered by commercial art galleries. Nothing as limiting as having to conform to coherent subject matter or to a recognizable period in the history of the arts. A collection of Trinidadian and Salvatore-masterpieces are displayed throughout the bar: the former consisting of Junkanoo processions of street musicians, and exotic floral arrangements featuring indigenous tropicals; the latter consisting of astral bodies hovering over surreal landscapes, another of an angel ascending above a stretch of highway. Now you tell me that there's no connection between the Ashley and the Divine. There is plentiful evidence to support this heretofore theory, now fact (ignoring Eve's uninvited commentary on all of this, of course). Mere coincidence, my ass. This place is built on an energy field that will make your wristwatch stick to your zipper, and make a lame man dance.

There is a significant literary, if not geographic, relationship between Stuart and the Moroccan city of romantic legend, Casablanca. *Yes, there is*. Perhaps not as closely related by latitude as Nixonville, South Carolina (Casablanca and Nixonville are latitudinal relatives), is to Casablanca.

Allow me to challenge your disbelief. Travel with me to the Ashley. If it helps, close your eyes. No, don't do that. Because you won't be able to read what comes next. Okay, wait. Read this first, and then do as you're instructed. Close your eyes (squeeze them so hard it makes you grin). Now imagine that this is Rick's Place, the cafe and clandestine gathering place for French refugees fleeing the Nazi occupation of their homeland. Here they flock, to Casablanca where they hope to book passage to a new life. They cling to the only thing they have left. Hope. They are like men and women huddled together in a crowded lifeboat. They await their rescue. Waiting for that ship or plane to arrive that will take them to the land of their dreams. To the place where they can begin their lives anew.

How like Casablanca, Stuart. And how like Rick's Place, the Ashley. The Ashley, a sanctuary for the disenfranchised. Refugees, nonetheless. Recent arrivals from the Midwest, Middle Atlantic and the Southern States. Fugitives, really, having escaped the brutal tyranny of child support payments, probation officers and the New York and Chicago mafia.

This huddled mass gathers at the Ashley in the time honored tradition with which America has always welcomed its immigrants. That is, no questions asked. If you did ask, would you really want to know? Particularly when the back story of the man or lady standing next to you at the bar began with: "Organized Crime Connected. Must

Report and Register with Local Law Enforcement;" "Cannibal – Deviant Appetite in Remission. Released from Bellevue (200 mg Abilify, x2 q.i.d.);" "NYPD- Medically Retired, full disability ([can't dance] shot self in foot)." Hey, whose business is it anyway? Maybe you too were inhumanely handled by your caretakers, or treated unjustly by the courts, or your vengeful spouse, or the IRS. Not eligible for a cot at Chrome Detention Center, or a new identity and a house in Port St. Lucie complements of the Witness Protection Program? Then Stuart's the place for you. If you are the exception and *can adjust* to the heat of the subtropics, *can dance*, and you look good in a thong, then you should move to Miami. If you don't meet any of the criteria then why not become a patron of the Ashley? Stand beneath the Seraphim angel holding the welcome-shaft of light. She is your Statue of Liberty. You are her tired, hungry and reluctant to learn to dance. You've come to the right place. You can start out with the hokey pokey and the Chicken Dance. Why, you might just do the hokey pokey and turn your life around. So don't you chicken out. Just hang in there and persevere. And I'm going to tell you how, but first a word from your wardrobe consultant.

CHAPTER 5

limbo to lindy, be bop & hip hop...
underwear optional, 'cept for kilt wearing Scots

What should I wear tonight?" "I don't have anything decent to go out in." Eve! I've heard her say this every time we've gone out since we were married. To include our wedding day, peculiar as that may sound, but I'll explain later. Well tonight was no exception. It hadn't been more than a month since our first visit to the area. That was the time when I first experienced my fear of dancing at the Ashley. Still imagining it to be the ghosted dance floor of the Titanic, with me and my partner sailing on a collision course with disaster. Fearing this still I feigned a hamstring injury. I wasn't truthful with Eve. I just said, "You look fine. You look as good in that dress as when you bought it." "Stewart! I bought this in Italy when I was pregnant with Angie." "Don't you have a belt that matches it?" "You can't wear a belt with an empire styled dress." "Then wear jeans and a blouse." "I don't have a nice blouse that'll go with my jeans." Well then...ask Angie if you can wear her red-neck shirt. The one that ties in the front." "That'll look stupid on me. I'm too old to be showing my midriff. My belly's getting flabby. I need to start doing sit-ups again... loose a few pounds." "What...now? Do you want me to hold your ankles and count for you? Can I get you a fat burner...want one or two?" "Shut up. Get out and let me get dressed." "Eve, Eve, Eve (giving myself time to think)...it doesn't matter what you wear. *We're just going to the Ashley.*

"What should you wear when you go dancing? Professional ballroom dancers are famous for their extensive and elaborate wardrobes. While we encourage you to dress up and have fun, make sure that you are comfortable and unencumbered. Wear clothes that permit freedom of movement. Women may prefer to wear heels when dancing, to help keep the weight of the body forward, on the balls of the feet, where most of the dance steps take place. Men should wear flexible, thin-soled shoes with a slight heel. Again, the heel helps to keep body weight forward. No matter what shoes you decide to wear, they should be comfortable and flexible."

From, "Shall We Dance?"
by, Manine Rosa Golden

Dance apparel? Not even an afterthought to the our bar patron. Strikingly unlike the Ballantray Country Club or the Rocking Horse Lounge where, without your jacket, tie, décolletage, or Justin boots and wranglers, you're an Ashley dancer who got lost and showed up at the wrong place. Maybe it's a case of *sartorial satori*; a matter of the meaninglessness of clothes to the illumined bhikku of the bar scene. They would rather be naked, wearing a barrel with shoulder straps, than wear an article of clothing with a designer label. I have never seen so many bad dressers in one place as at the Ashley. I know it's not kind to say anything offensive about what other people wear. But I'm talking about the sensory over-load of seeing horizontal and vertical patterns on the same outfit. Now, I admit to poor color coordination due to congenital color blindness. I can dress under a spotlight and be color-mismatched just the same as if I'd dressed in a dark closet with the door shut. Often have I heard Eve or Angie shriek, "Stewart, you look like you shopped at a Lithuania thrift store. That orange shirt doesn't match the khaki's." My son, Zack, whose less inclined to insult me with ethnic slurs (and who obviously hasn't inherited my color blindness), dryly comments, "Dad, you look like a flamingo. You'd look really good standing on the front lawn." I always heed their wardrobe wisdom. I change before I can embarrass myself in public. That is if they're home when I get dressed. If not I try to keep a low profile and travel at night.

You won't see an Ashley visitor keeping a low profile. They are very high profile people for want of a better way to describe their flash and pizzazz. Remember the guy I told you about earlier. The one with the 2/4 fade tribal tattoos and the baseball cap with the crown shaped like an orange carp? Yep, real. I saw him there, and I have sober witnesses who will confirm the sighting. However, I wouldn't be surprised if he no longer exists. His personal identity has probably been deleted from the national data bank. Possibly beamed back to a fish camp in a distant galaxy, or given a new hat and a new identity and residing in Port St. Lucie. Certainly, not everyone is as flamboyant as lagoon man. Some are...well, stand outs in other significant ways. Like the woman in the red dress for example. Her name - if my memory doesn't fail me - was, ah...Carmen Maria Esmeralda Silverstein. Don't let a name fool you. She could have played the double for Kelly LeBrock, the *Woman in Red*. To Eve, she was a "working woman" taxi dancing for dimes. And you know what surprises me? I don't remember Eve having ever so judgmental. Maybe it was because Carmen, the lady in the red dress, had forgotten her under-garments. Braless as was evident by the chill test and panty-less by the exposure caused by her dance partner's gymnastic skills. Every time what's-his-name spun her, hoisted her and dipped her she auditioned for Basic Instinct. Our table commanded an excellent ring side view of the dance floor. Seated at our table with us were our friends, Bob and Claire. It was their initiation to the Ashley. They responded to the vibes like Ashley homies. When Carmen and what's-his-name danced, Bob and I acted discrete, trying to maintain an aplomb of good manners and passive attention. The women (I'd refer to them as girls, but the reference is sexist and politically incorrect) were blunt and catty the way women can be when a stray, wayward sort of woman wearing nothing but a mink stole wanders into a pack of militant feminists who are also animal rights activists. Eve pointed to Carmen, leaned over to whisper something into Claire's ear. I overheard her say something to the effect that Carmen's buns were the consistency of bread left out in the rain, and that she could never make a living as a hot dog vender. With cavalier grace I interjected, "she dances well doesn't she?" I knew the moment the words had left my mouth that I had spoken blasphemy. Eve, at least knew, that I knew that no one here could dance. And that the only thing of aesthetic interest to me was Carmen's glorious ass. Well Claire, noticing the storm clouds in Eve's eyes, interrupted with, "Eh, she's wearing a thong", as if to say, the woman would be overdressed at a nudists' camp. Claire's talent for equivocation was challenged when, Carmen executing a dance maneuver with her partner that looked like the limbo, showed the editor's uncut version.

I abruptly remarked that the orchid displayed in the Trinidadian art work that hung over our table was a pink Phalaenopsis. This was an observation that intrigued Eve and our friends, and made them study the painting with the déjà vu of familiar recognition. I gazed on it long, thinking to myself, how life at the Ashley imitates the art.

My focus here, mind you, is not on fashion frills. A night at this bar is no fashion show, but it is a cattle call; in the sense of prospective models being called to a location for a camera shoot. However these photo-fatales are not registered with any of the elite modeling agencies. Some are not even registered with Immigration. They are nonetheless "beautiful people," if you subscribe to my mother's dictum that, it's what's inside a person that counts.' I personally don't want to go there right now. The prospect of sorting through the individual differences of an evolving new species rekindles the tedium that I associate with college taxonomy, combined with the costume and make-up artistry achieved by Lucas Film Productions. I once believed that 'clothes made the man.' That is until I witnessed the week-end fashion parade at the Ashley. And why there, and not down the street, say, at the Black Marlin or the Flagler Grille? Places where people are dressed fashionably, gender congruent and more or less color and pattern coordinated. Because one of the most celebrated, historical characters after whom the Ashley is named was a notorious bank robber and a cross-dresser. On this note I'll tell you about *the other famous bank robbery.*

Now you know about the first bank hold-up. The one that in occurred in 1915, and was committed by John and Bob Ashley and Kid Lowe. You also remember that it was the Kid's bad temper and his quick trigger finger that set John to hopping about in pain, thus setting the example for the future of Ashley dancing.

The second robbery occurred in May, 1922. The newspaper reported that, Hanford Mobley, nephew of John Ashley, dressed as a woman and with two accomplices held up the bank for a few thousand dollars. Eventually the three were caught in Plant city. And it wasn't that Hanford was all that pretty that he could pass for a woman. His blue-black five o'clock shadow, and his thick arms and unshaven legs did not present a picture of refined, feminine delicacy. It is said that it was the crop of chest hair that sprung from the neck line of his high-collared dress, and the baritone voice commanding the teller to hand over the loot that gave Hanford away. The women customers in the bank spotted him as a phony from the start, noticing immediately that his purse and shoes didn't match.

So, large men in drag performing in a trocadero skit can be traced to the indigenous culture of this town. I once looked in Angie's eighth grade Florida Studies textbook. And because it was the politically corrected, multi-culturally sensitive revisionist edition, I found a thousand mea culpa for every White American transgression against everyone who was *not*. But I tell you, nowhere, I repeat, nowhere, was there one apology, or whisper of, "I'm sorry," for what John Ashley and Hanford Mobley did to haberdashery and dance. In fact they are regarded as heroes, albeit American mythological anti-heroes, shamelessly revered for their deranged antics.

Sadly though, the descendants of the Ashleys and the Mobleys hide their names in shame. Ada Coats Williams who wrote a book entitled, "Florida's Ashley Gang," reported that the shamed scions of these erstwhile bandits did change their names. Having done so in order to evade the unwanted attention of the Stuart Times paparazzi, Bert Reynolds talent scouts, and to discourage the unsolicited proposals of marriage from the Florida women's' chapter of "Pen Pals to Prisoners." Reputedly only one member of these two families retained his true name. This was Bill Mobley, the younger brother of Hanford. He is now deceased, God rest his soul. He is purported to have said to Ada, at the close of her interview with him, "Why reopen the wounds? None of the children could bear to carry the pain of the name; now they have different names. None of the bodies could rest in their graves; vandals and ghouls desecrated each one - there's not a bone in any of them." Pusillanimous offspring, family turncoats, and next-of-kin grave robbers? Just another strong influence upon the current, popular epidemic of self-loathing and public confessions daily exposed by the national media. Enough of the ancestor bashing, The scions of the Stuart founding fathers have a right to their genealogical denial. I have no right as an outsider to cast aspersions on their...um, well... strangeness. They didn't choose their ancestry. In fact, most of the undesirable traits identified have been camouflaged by the weird idiosyncrasies expressed by the outsiders. I realize that there is a limit to what the nonfiction reader will tolerate when handicapped people are being bashed. I am sincere in saying: I am looking optimistically to the near future (wishful thinking) when these caste, clan and regional differences will fade into benign and tolerable quirkiness. My intention is not to malign the less fortunate and the unattractive. Besides, it's the Ashleys and Mobleys business if they choose to hide behind Hanford's petticoats. Why immigrants still do it; change their name that is. My neighbor, a.k.a., Bud Toby, is really Boris Toblinkinoskai.

Bud, the Cassock, changed his name when he emigrated from the Steps of Russia fifty years ago. Bud is mostly bald with the exception of a long pony-tail that he wears in a braid. He also raises wolf hounds as a hobby. See, you can't hide genes behind a name change. Like the Toblinkinoskais, the Ashleys and the Mobleys are among us. They are disproportionately represented in the demographic of the town and, moreover, at the Ashley. Try and hide it they may, but no matter how hard they try, or might try and fake it...it's quite obvious, they just can't dance.

    A week-end at the Ashley is a perpetual celebration honoring their deeds. Their ghosts are conjured up each year at the Stuart Downtown "Dancing in the Street" celebration. During the week-end festivities the robbery of the former bank is re-enacted by the owners of the Ashley. Hoss Dodge or one of the buff and burley bouncers dresses as Hanford posing as a woman. Patrons are, faithful to historic accuracy, relieved of their valuables. The re-enacted robbery becomes street entertainment as the acting gangsters burst through the doors of the Ashley, and then back into the street, guns blazing. The crowd cheers, drinking continues, and the frisked and empty-pocketed patrons are left to wonder if their losses will be credited to their checks. There you have it, living history. The Ashley gang immortalized. Over the years, deed and drag have become... the sacred ritual and holy robes of the venerable bhikkus of the downtown bar scene.

This is not a tribute to fashion or a guide to etiquette. These elements, though, set the Ashley's patrons apart from the herd. They are a social experiment. And every new social experiment and non-violent revolution has its generation. A generation determined to set itself apart from the social mainstream that it perceives as mired in traditions which have become mundane and meaningless. History has documented the movements, and the revolutions that historians want the masses to remember. I have read somewhere that, 'History is the certainty produced at the point where the imperfections of memory meet the inadequacies of documentation.' Since most of the customers I've talked to haven't read a history book, they aren't likely to repeat any of it. Such was the wisdom conveyed in Santayana's admonition that we should learn from history's unsuccessful events so as not to repeat them. The regulars of the Ashley may create brand new, never before made mistakes. And yet what we may prejudge as mistakes might in fact be innovations. Innovative ways to correct the missed-steps and stumbling others may perceive as their inability to dance.

This change is not set in motion by something as dramatic as the 'shot heard round the world.' Not anything as explosive as a volcanic upheaval spewing molten lava to immolate the old order in the cleansing fires of nature's or society's retribution. No fife, drum or cannonade to announce the coming of the freedom dancers. No, it's more like the repetitive finger tapping and the ho hum murmurings of boredom. This is a quiet, non-violent social revolution. Best described in the expressive Italian vernacular, *dolce far niente*...happening through 'the sweetness of doing nothing.' That sublime state of "being one with the moment". Or, just, 'hanging with your buds' if you'd prefer. What an extraordinarily subtle revolution in contrast to the violent upheavals occurring elsewhere in the world. These are the first people since the Hippies to actually 'go with the flow.' And the very first established group who never rafted, so to speak, in the rapids of the social mainstream to begin with. 'Going with the flow' is like tubing down the lazy river for an Ashleyite. What might resemble an involuntary reflex similar to an epileptic seizure set to music is a cake walk compared to the danse macabre of the Arab Spring. The revolutionary slogan of this Brave New Culture? Here it is as I heard it chanted to the drum beat of Bolero. And I can say this unabashedly; it made me proud.

Okay, it went like this, 'Hell no, we won't dance. We won't dance the Waltz.' And everyone should know that the Waltz has been performed longer than any other ballroom dance. This is deviance unequaled in the history of dance.

There is no standard uniform into which the Ashley patron is fitted for the week-end muster. No weapons are permitted, although Eve said she wouldn't object to some airport security at the Ashley. I know this harks back to Eve's airline days. She was an Eastern Airlines flight attendant in the days before passengers were patted down and strip searched to make them feel safer about flying. I still remember having panic attacks back then over not knowing if the Middle Eastern looking passenger seated next to me with the bulge under his pant fly was a U.S. Air Marshall with brass balls or Jaffar the Underwear Bomber. Now, TSA is there to make me feel a lot better about boarding the same Stretch DC 8 to which Eve was assigned as Chief Flight Attendant in 1974. As for the Ashley, I have to admit that a body scanner and a conveyor system that fluoroscopes and examines carry-ons would make us both feel a little safer. Take Trish for example. We met her at the pool table last Saturday night. We happened to meet because we were the next pile of four quarters next to the guy's stack of quarters who she beat. This is pool playing etiquette's equivalent to being on stand-by for an over-booked flight at the airport (to further the airport analogy). Trish was a pool dancer. Which means that whether she shot or waited her turn she grooved to the music. Trish was dressed in the uniform of the Black Velvet Republican Army. She was built like a chess pawn with long curvaceous legs. She was squeezed into a black velvet skirt; the kind you're tempted to pet, but don't because you're too smart to risk a pool stick injury or a knee to the groin. So I admired the fabric. The way that an art aficionado appraises the black velvet canvases on which Mexican artists paint Elvis, the Madonna and Sacred Heart Jesus. Well Trish was no Mother-of-God Madonna. She told me she was an ex-biker chick whose iron horseman moved to Manhattan to accept a seat on the New York Stock Exchange. He told her that there was no longer room for her on the saddle of his Harley. Besides, said Trish, with enough English on the next shot to land the cue ball in the lap of a guy seated at a nearby table, "He traded his custom Sportster in on a Lexus, bought a dozen long sleeve shirts to hide his tats, and left me with the memorable parting words, 'Hey babe, people change. ' "The fuck'n sell out!" Here was the twice crowned Queen of Top Dog Cafe's Bike Night. Making her debut at the Ashley. There in high heels, wearing her first skirt in fifteen years, and just drunk enough to hide the melancholy, put on the attitude and miss every other shot. I commented to Eve that you had to admire Trish's courage in leaving the pack, and venturing into the Ashley. Coming here to find herself, and about to realize that finding yourself in this place isn't going to happen. This subliminal realization was apparent in the too-big smile worn by Trish that night. It stayed on her lips throughout her pool table tango, displayed wide enough at times to show the gap between her top front teeth. Faking happiness with her best Lauren Hutton smile. Eve, with genuine female empathy, keened softly, saying to Trish, "Walter's lost the best pool partner he'll ever have. He deserves to be devoured by the vicious concrete chasm of Wall Street." I asked Eve how she knew his name was Walter. To which Eve replied, "Why, Stewart, your great powers of observation must be failing you. I noticed Trish's tattoo when she bent over to make that difficult bank shot." "Oh, you mean the red heart and flaming orange banner. Is that what it said?"

CHAPTER 6

birds of a feather flock together

A Friday night gathering at the Ashley is like double booking an Audubon Society ornithology exhibition and a Treky convention. And no one is really sure of from what genus, species, or corner of the galaxy the colorful creature standing next to you might have come. Doesn't even matter. Far be it that anyone should ask. Because the Ashley patron ignores the formalities of social convention. Such as cordial introductions – in the manner by which two strangers get to know one another. Why normally, a friendly first encounter might typically begin with Stranger #1 saying to Stranger #2, "Gee, I'm a Virgo, you must be an Aries." To which Stranger #2 (wearing a ram head medallion the size of an aircraft searchlight), might reply, "My God you must be psychic. How'd ya know?" Then off to the parking lot for a blow job. At the Ashley a social phobia imitating a talent for still- life modeling guarantees protected and safe social intercourse. I assume that not all of the venerable bhikkus have taken the vow of celibacy. But I can't imagine any of them making it as far as the parking lot in tandem. I tested my assumption by sharing my thoughts on it with Eve. She said that my correspondence course in sex therapy didn't license me to concoct theories about the locals. I stood corrected. Even so, Eve and I agreed that the poor dance performances we had been witnessing were a mating ritual. No parking lot trysts necessary. Boy, did I feel embarrassed for having judged these bouncing, whirling, dance hall dervishes so critically on the basis of their dancing skills alone. Me, of all people, who couldn't execute a glide across the dance floor with the help of a Hollywood studio motorized dance platform.

> "The clear, simple steps of the Waltz produce a smooth pattern that will allow you to glide gently around the dance floor in no time."
>
> From, "Shall We Dance?"
> By, Manine Rosa Golden

To Manine: I wave the battle flag, and I pound my chest and say..."Hell no. I won't dance. I won't dance the Waltz!" Or if honesty is the virtue you desire...I can't dance the Waltz.

This is not a manual on dance or a bird guide. It is a treatise on the mating behaviors of a Brave New Culture – perhaps lacking coordination but not lacking in sex hormones. These people seem to have little desire to screw by ordinary means. This is because the reproductive organs of such sentient, post moderns is reductivistic. And *their* approach is that they will use their reproductive apparatus when they are capable of collectively imagine their existence and figure out where and to what use to put them. I trust that someday they will discover more constructive and less frivolous uses to which most of us now put them. This doesn't mean that the Ashley mate-seeker lacks passion - maybe rhythm and balance - but not passion. For passion will build like an electrical charge in the superconductive atmosphere of the bar. Once one learns to dance, then surely passion, like storm lightning, will follow.

"The Tango reflects the passionate, exciting music to which it is danced. While there are many dazzling sequences that can be added to this dance, the basic steps are easy to learn. The drama lies in the smooth, florid execution of the steps and the slow, tense rhythms of the music... Be conservative while learning this dance; do not exaggerate your movements. The tango - known as the dance of love - should be danced in a closed hold.

From, "Shall We Dance?"
By, Manine Rosa Golden

"Smooth, and florid execution...Be conservative...Don't exaggerate your movements." These instructions are converted to antonymic corruptions deep within the central nervous system of the nocturnal dancer. It's a phenomenon that is produced by forces that are beyond the conscious control of the dancer. Lessons can teach the novice to dance, but the nature of the Ashley dancer won't let it happen. An Ashley dancer can no more control his movements than can the chicken just be-headed by a hatchet. Why? Wouldn't you expect that someone who graduated magna cum laude from the Alvin Ailey School of Ballet and Modern Dance would be a stand-out dancer anywhere? Well that's what I expected from Johnnie and Theresa Valenzuela when they debuted at the Ashley. Eve, Claire, Bob and I had gotten their verbal vitae after striking up a table-next-to-theirs conversation. That's when we learned that Johnnie and Theresa met at the fine arts academy, danced into one another's arms and remained in the dancers close hold forever like slimy annelids. Claire found this out about them in a record five minutes. Claire has this way of turning a conversation with a stranger into an interrogation. I've seen her at work, and what always amazes me is that rather than getting defensive or acting bullied, her chosen victims become inveterate confessors. They probably think they're being interviewed by a Jerry Springer talent scout. And the people who really pique Claire's interest are the ones who sport a bolder image than the rest, if you catch my drift. Like Johnnie and Theresa. This was a couple that gets noticed. You know what I mean. Here's this crowded bar and in walk the Valenzuelas. The crowd gathered around the main entrance parts like the Red Sea. A momentary hush falls over the crowd. Eyes snatch brief glimpses and compare them to memory like an eye-witness searching through police photographs, fashion magazines, or the tabloids for a hint of recognition. This all takes place in a micro-second. Conversations continue. The crowd is animated once more. And people are left to wonder...who were those svelte, androgynous athletic types who looked like Mr. and Mrs. Super-Duo in Lycra lights? These are times when I truly connect with Claire, and can relate to her playful Torquemada curiosity.

It torments her not to know everything there is to know about *individuals* like the Valenzuelas. Claire and Eve were fascinated by their mystique (the one Claire manufactured), while Bob and I remained aloof, each of us privately imagining what each other would look like in lycra tights and grinning stupidly. The spell, if you could call it that, was broken soon enough when Johnnie invited Theresa to dance. They cast an aren't-you going-to-join-us look in our direction...and got absolutely no response. I knew and so did the others that their dance expertise, no matter how natural or professionally drilled, couldn't prevail against the forces at work beneath the dance floor of the Ashley. The Valenzuelas were in trouble and they didn't even know it. They wouldn't know what had befallen them until...it was too late. Johnnie's confidence was the first to crumble. His sudden, herky-jerky motions caused Theresa to recoil. She backed away four steps, far enough for another couple to come between them. And there was Johnnie with the twitching heebie jeebies - dancing solo. Then it must have come to Johnnie - the same way it must have struck Rumi the Sufi after a fit of whirling - that a man dancing badly and alone in Lycra tights is a sight for sore eyes. This dreaded moment of clarity was Johnnie's undoing. Not only had his lifelong annelid peeled herself off and abandoned him, but so had his ability to dance.

No mere words could console the mortified Valenzuelas. Certainly none that either could offer the other, because they weren't speaking to one another. I couldn't help but feel responsible for possibly ruining their marriage, their dance partnership...or whatever. I knew afterwards that I should have warned them. Eve reassured me later that they wouldn't have understood if I had tried to explain it to them. She said they would have thought I was crazy, and wouldn't have been entirely wrong. She added that it wasn't worth me embarrassing her in front of the Valenzuelas. And that although they had had an unfortunate experience, they'd just have to heal the shame, and let go of their pride like I had. Here was Eve being uncharacteristically callus...again. I became co-dependent and tried to offer excuses for Johnnie. I said, "Hey John (trying to make him feel more grown up), maybe you're coming down with the bug that's going around. I had it last month. It messes with your balance; causes this weird vestibular disorder. Why, every time I rose to stand, the damn room would start spinning and I'd lose my balance." "Yeah, maybe you're right. I did feel a little dizzy when I got up to dance with Theresa. What did you do about it?" " My doctor gave me a prescription for Antivert, and, ah...he told me to lay off dancing for a while. Especially here at the Ashley..." At which time Eve rudely interrupted, "Stewart don't give medical advice. And don't go there." I got her hint. And after a long minute of heavy silence we said good night to the still morose Valenzuelas. Leaving them there to ponder their relationship, a career change, and what they would look like in business suits.

"Cafes and coffeehouses are more than just weigh stations: they are both havens from the workplace and substitutes for it. Hemingway, Simone de Beauvoir, Sartre, and multitudes of other writers, both acclaimed and unknown, have written novels, treatises, and poems in cafes with a cup of coffee at their elbow."

From, "Espresso"
By, Petzke & Slavin

Don't get the idea that I spend all of my time at the Ashley. Or that I partake of the nightlife, nightly. Does anyone? No one that I know over the age of forty has the constitutional fitness for it, or can really tolerate the repetitive sameness. Not that there aren't the exceptions. I have known the Ashley to be the home away from home to some whose occupations have yet to be entered in the Dictionary of Occupational Titles. They generally leave when the doors of Fellowship Hall open for the 'Lunch Bunch' AA meeting. Some of the stragglers will help keep the stools bolted to the floor and catch the 7:30 p.m. 'Open' meeting. And anyone left will maintain they are receiving all the support they need right there, and will save themselves a trip across the street. After all the Ashley is a restaurant by day. Breakfast and lunch is served during the season, and week-end brunch features mid-morning orange juice cocktails that are guaranteed to put sunshine into almost any occasion, even on the rainiest day. I prefer the local Java Joint for morning espresso; desiring the dark juice of the Arabica coffee cherry. A drink that Eve says I over-romanticize, and who said to me after a sip from the demitasse that it was an experience that compared with swapping tobacco spit with a Marlins pitcher. It was the next day - on a Saturday - that I stopped by the Ashley on the pretense of searching for the muse of inspiration in the quiet of the day. The truth was that I was curious to see who was there, and to prove the null hypothesis that the interesting people probably only came out at night. I also couldn't face a tiny cup of hot tobacco spit (after Eve spoiled it for me) at the Java Joint which *had been* my Saturday morning routine. So I visited the Ashley in the light of early morning half expecting to walk through Transylvania dirt, and find the living dead napping on the dance floor. To my surprise, and relief, everything appeared... normal. There was the usual bustle associated with getting ready for the day's business. Waiters and waitresses were arriving, putting on clean white aprons, filling salt and pepper shakers, and topping off the sugar bowls. Bartenders stocked the bar. And the cook staff stocked the kitchen larders. Hoss and Annie interrupted their chores to greet me. It was one of those busy hellos crowded with distractions. You know, a hurried, 'hello', and a 'how are you,' followed by a vanishing act. Hoss reappeared a moment later, bringing me a scrapbook to study. It contained newspaper clippings, old photographs and magazine articles that told the Ashley's history. I sat at the bar, took out my pen and notepad, and ordered a coffee...a pale Robusta brew into which I poured half as much cream, a tablespoon of sugar and dropped in an ice cube. A retro-scene isn't it? From which you might expect the extemporaneous creation of culturally Avant Guard prose, post-modern epic poetry, or something brand new and fresh on the literary scene. After all, existentialism, feminism, and the modern novel were from inspired artists and writers who frequented the bars and cafes of Paris in the early decades of the last century. Ever since, the written word has grown quieter and quieter as the voice for new ideas has grown silent. And my exercises in writing on this particular day at the Ashley, I dreaded to think, would contribute materially to the decline of worthwhile ideas, and hasten the death of the novel. Specifically, the one that I'd just begun a month ago. Eve told me that this was a vain conceit because others much more talented than me had killed it long ago. I would have to condescend to sharing the blame with real literary war criminals whose atrocities I could only hope to imitate. After all what's been written of late that isn't derivative, formulaic, or some nobody's memoir? Maybe Eve was right (as always), and I was being grandiose. What's more, what could be here that's worth writing about? That's the hopeless I was beginning to feel...just before what the noon-day was about to reveal. For when the blinding light coming through the plate glass window grew darker as the waiter lowered the awnings - in walked the spirits of Allen Ginsberg, Lawrence Ferlinghetti, Gary Snyder, Bob Kaufman and my favorite, and original, Beat writer and bar bhikku, Jack , a.k.a. Dulouz Kerouac. They all looked impossibly young, good in berets, and sober. Yes, even I was worried that I had deluded myself and had entered the zone introduced and made famous by Rod Serling. But it turned out to be four sisters and their friend from Maryland arriving at the lunch hour. Coming through the doors and bathed in a nimbus of bright sunshine. I'm addicted to sunglasses and I realized too late that I should have been wearing them. Everyone knows how the sun can play tricks on you. I tried to explain this to Eve, who reminded me that mirages generally appear as pools of water to the thirsty traveler in the desert, and normally not as apparitions to a coffee drinker at a restaurant or bar. She also asked how I knew they were sisters, and wasn't at all interested in thinking of them as literary spirit guides as I had. I tried to explain that unlike the typically shy late night Ashley patron these daytime types were a lot more sociable, and that I, or they (I couldn't remember who broke the ice), just struck up a conversation. I submitted, perhaps unwisely, that they may have been induced to open up a bit more than usual due to the high doses of Prozac that their psychiatrist had prescribed. Most likely the combination of a potent mood brightener and the energy field surrounding the Ashley was powerful enough to 'call' these women to Stuart all the way from Maryland. Their explanation was that they were here for an Orioles game, and to take in a few rounds of golf. The eldest sister, Margaret, by way of having introduced herself as senior among them, spoke on about how they had been staying at their parent's condominium. And how they happened upon Stuart's historic downtown, wandered into the Ashley, were taking a break from the children, were bonding as sisters and healing from the childhood abuses inflicted upon them by their father whom all four sisters were now prepared to forgive - all of this on the advice of their therapists. This brief, informal out-patient consultation was encouraged unwittingly by having told Margaret that I was a psychologist in private practice. It's the same sort of thing that happens to anyone willing to listen to the airline passenger seated next to them on a long, tedious flight. And when I told her that the notes that I had been gathering at the bar was research for a book of modest, yet great sociological importance, she made me promise to mention her and her sisters and their friend. So here it is, as promised, and without the customary consent allowing me to release confidential information. And what's noteworthy about my encounter with these women was not their story. Their story is worn out tabloid news. It was their epiphany at the Ashley, and to the sodium-pentathol-effect this place has on the deaf, dumb, and deeply repressed. Most impressive was their undaunted courage to open up and have their confessions heard by a total stranger. Not a moment after having been cleansed of a life-time of guilt and shame, they were soiled by the untoward advances of Ben and Harry. It was the youngest sister, Terry, who became the target of Ben's...laser pointer. Ben and Harry are basically harmless regulars who were, as usual, irrigating their parched gullets while employing their asses as full-time stool warmers. Ben's indiscretion was having used his laser pointer inappropriately. He carried it in his shirt pocket, crammed among the pens and mechanical pencils of his crowed pocket protector. If you couldn't guess, Ben is an out-of-work aerospace engineer with time on his hands. Chalk it up to boredom or lust, because Terry sat there looking like Jamie Lee Curtis doing an underwear commercial. Ben had the laser pointer in hand, finger on the on-button and the beam on Terry's substantial boob. And if you've seen a laser pointer, you know they emit a sneaky form of light. There's no beam, per se, by which to trace the source. Because it focuses a spot of red light on its target, and for all you know it could have originated from the moon. Before Terry noticed what was happening, Ben's red dot had been dancing lasciviously across Terry's chest; tracing double "D" diameter circles, stopping on the left nipple, then the right nipple, and when it reached Terry's navel and began to traveling to the lower regions of her anatomy she saw it, saw Ben, and gave him a *look* followed by the clear spoken message, "You asshole, what are you doing? I'd like to aim that thing at your crotch, and cauterize your dick, you idiot." To which Ben retorted, "I am not an idiot. I'm only temporarily out of work. Grumman is down-sizing. Besides this is a low powered laser. It doesn't cause burns...though it could damage your retina if it were aimed..." "Shut the fuck up! And yes, you are an idiot." I could see that Terry's therapy was paying off. She certainly wasn't lacking in assertiveness or confrontational skills. Nonetheless, she was humiliated and pissed off. She left to get a blouse from her park car, and put it on to cover her laser violated torso. She moved to the end of the bar closer to where I was seated. She was wise to keep her distance from Ben the menace. Finding comfort, I supposed, near a man whose pen was... just a pen, and who probably represented the father she had idealized and never had. This was the plausible-sounding Freudian analysis. This is precisely how I described the interlude later to Eve during my interrogation. She has very little tolerance for a sound theoretical argument. "Don't try to sell me that Freudian father-figure crap. I know a Freudian fraud when I see one. And besides Freud's cigar wasn't just a cigar, and neither was Clinton's." That hurt. So I decided to shut up while I was ahead. My Ashley daytime visit was an eye opener. Not to mention, a refutation of my null hypothesis. I told the Maryland pilgrims that they should come back at night when the Bens and Harrys turned into the Puerto Rican Princes, and all that was obscene was the dancing. I tried to reassure her, by letting her know that the patrons were required to check their laser pointers in at the door. Although I didn't venture out myself that evening, I could tell from their reaction to my invitation that they most likely didn't either.

As I have said, this is not a dance manual or a bird guide. However...there is a correlation if you think about it. This relationship is perhaps unique to the Ashley. You would have seen it for yourself had been there on a band night. You'd have observed first-hand the dance patterns of those, who, without fear of public censure, threw their motion to the music, and their caution to the wind.

Speaking of the wind, the tropical trade winds are the lofting and descending currents on which these Ashley patrons like birds, end their long migrations. The bands must have sent out imitative mating calls to which the far off flocks responded. The forces at work (remember the planetary grid lines?) beneath the Ashley guided their final approach. Nothing, however, seemed to help with the landings. I was there. I witnessed the arrival of the bar Kamikaze; bar flies with the grace of flying pigs and the aerobatic skills of domestic turkeys.

"Why do some birds migrate at night and others travel during the day?"

"How do birds that have never migrated before know when to leave and where to go?"

"How does a tiny warbler cross 2000 miles of ocean in a nonstop flight lasting more than two days?"

>Questions asked and answered in,
>How Birds Migrate,
>by Paul Kerlinger

Why do some patrons migrate to the Ashley at night and others travel there during the day?

How do bar flies that have never migrated before know how to find their way to the Ashley?

How is a 5',2", 105 lb. divorcee without food or gas money able to drive 2000 miles from Buffalo to Stuart in two days?

>Questions asked and answered in,
>The Ashley by,
>Roland Verfaillie

I've answered the first two questions already. But how does that dainty divorcee make it on such meager resources? Like the angels or the warblers? Not likely. Being an apterous biped she had to depend on her beat up '76 Oldsmobile to make it here. Couldn't she have drafted behind semis the entire trip? Is that the answer? Who knows? I could speculate, that the fear of Harold, her ex-spouse and stalker, was the motivator. Perhaps she had to appeal to the kindness of the knights of the road, or tank up and take off at the gas pumps. Maybe there's more to it than mere reason can explain. Since Stuart, and ultimately the Ashley, was her final destination – and she wasn't very forthcoming when asked how she did it – I stopped guessing. Dealing with problems, and mysteries that science has pondered for centuries becomes a no-brainer (a redundancy) when you simply surrender to faith. By the simple act of not thinking too deeply, you too can turn out great literature like those geniuses did who wrote *A Course in Miracles*, *The Celestine Prophecy*, and *The Twilight Series*.

We can leave it to these inspired thinkers supply the answer as to how "How that divorcee did it." The answer I was told is metaphysically self-evident: It was by pure animal magnetism. She was attracted to others of her kind. And, thanks to a diet high in iron she was drawn...no, pulled forcibly, and at great velocity to Stuart - which, you remember, is situated on a geocentric energy nexus. This is not that farfetched, when you consider that this is a bone fide scientific theory for how pigeons navigate long distances. So, as the theory goes, she was drawn to others like herself. Now those of a familiar feather - of the human variety - are not as conspicuous as, say, painted birds, easy to identify by their paint-by-number patterns, or song birds with their signature melodies. So how does one pair up or group with others of their human kind? It's too easy to settle on the fact that opposites attract. We all know about the laws of magnetic attraction. And we erroneously apply these laws to human bonding. Gender's one thing, but there are so many other variables that just don't figure so easily. Not in the same way the laws of physics and mechanics might. Take, for example, when the alcoholic and co-dependent or the compulsive over-eater and the anorectic hook up. These kinds of relationships can work if they are driven by supply side economics where each person in the relationship shares his or her surplus with the other. Patrons of the Ashley, on the other hand, are searching for genuinely compatible relationships. And the criteria by which they are attempting to match up are unimaginably difficult. Because finding a match involves finding that man or woman whose hop, skip, jump, dip and pelvic swivel is synchronous to the beat of the music that only you and him and no one else can see, hear or feel. It's the trial and error which results that Eve and I have witnessed since we began frequenting the Ashley. If the Valenzuelas hadn't drifted apart on the dance floor that evening and Johnnie hadn't lost his bearings they might still be in dance and dyadic syncopation today. But perhaps they weren't meant to live happily ever after. Because the forces at work within the Ashley will send your nervous system into overdrive. This could be nature's way of pulling incompatible couples apart. Even doing them a favor. Or, worse, what if even the compatible couples are repelled by sinister forces at work? Think about how a microwave oven works. You put a perfectly good egg inside, turn it on for a minute and what have you got? A lump of rearranged egg molecules with the flavor and texture of a Frisbee.

On first visiting the Ashley, my brother, Rick, instantly sensed the atmospheric disturbances and observed their even more disturbing effect on the customers. He was dumb struck over the scene on the dance floor. He found the words to say, 'Jesus Christ, no one here can dance.' Followed by further qualifying, 'No two couples are dancing the same dance. This is unbelievable. I thought my eyes were playing tricks on me. I mean after the Sambuca doubles, and the tequila shots, I thought my perception may have become, you know, a little distorted." No. I'm seeing the same thing," I quipped. "Hey bro, thanks for the reality check." And Rick has this gift for detecting subtle anomalies. Even noticing quondam shifts in the quantum force field. He doesn't depend on second sight, or on channeling expert spirit guides for their advice on important scientific matters like I do. I don't know how he does it, but he usually gets it right. He's the manager of an up-scale eatery in Miami. So seeing first-hand how *the others* struggle to get by must have been a shock for him. In the land of the nouveau-Conquistadors Rick goes by, "Richard"; an affectation upon which he insists in order to create a Ricardo Montelbon persona. Better, he thought, than the 'Rick' of *Rick's Place* in *Casa Blanca*. A tough -on-the-dames, Bogie persona is anathema in the 21st century. Not long ago he contemplated fleeing to Buenos Aires to evade the litigious talons of his last Bacall. And here is a guy who once upon a time wore a white linen suit with vest and bell bottom pants, raised his right arm high, pointed his index finger to the sky...and danced the disco.

"Disco fever swept the globe in 1978...and suddenly the nightclub subculture of America's urban gays and blacks hit the mainstream...The disco style broke with the rebellious sixties aesthetic that still dominated much of the youth culture. Men wore flashy suits and gold chains; women wore dresses and high heels. Couples danced together, to prescribed steps...A heavy throbbing rhythm ruled...lyrics centered on sex and its metaphors...What made disco vital, however, was a roomful of flamboyant, ecstatically dancing revelers."

> From, <u>Our Times:</u>
> <u>The Illustrated History</u>
> <u>of the 20th Century</u>
> Editor in Chief, Lorraine Glennon

Admittedly, I too danced to the yabyum of the disco. And I have a confession to make: I owned the white linen suit, not Rick. I feel ashamed for having turned my back on the sixties; for having deserted the Monkeys to follow the Bee Gees. But, alas, now we are all mired in the era of grunge, and we long for our exodus. The owners of the Ashley offered us all the opportunity to ease our tortured contortions and bend to a new limbo with the bow-legged, double jointed dexterity of Tattoo the midget. You would think it would involve 'raising the bar' higher. For once, maybe I'm wrong. How will this transformation happen? Okay, here's a hint in the form of a trivia question. What was the setting for the movie, "They Shoot Horses Don't They?" And I'm not talking about Kid Lowe's cruel treatment of animals or the Ashley's dinner menu. For the time being, you'll have to bear the suspense. Because, Hoss's and Annie's motive for providing *this opportunity* needs to be developed further. More of the key players need to be introduced. Eve was honest-to-god disappointed that I didn't have any idea as to what the owner's motives were. When I told her I'd have to give this some deep thought, and that I might even have to ask Hoss and Annie outright in my customary straightforward manner, her only comment was, "Yowza! Yowza! Yowza!" Not meaning to hurt her Spartan feelings, I told her she was, "warm, warm, very, very warm", but only in terms of getting closer to correctly answering the trivia question.

CHAPTER 7

return of "the dance-away lover"

In 1978 I splurged and bought the book, <u>The Dance-Away Lover</u>. I paid $1.95 for it on an annual salary of thirteen thousand dollars. I read it, and was so impressed that I kept it around for handy reference. It had dwelt in the vertical stack of books piled on my night stand, then stowed away in a storage crate, and finally in a book case nested among the countless books I've accumulated over the years. Its crooked spine now pokes out from a small book shelf in my office where it has become an obscure title among the dozens of pop psychology and self-help books of its generation. It has recently enjoyed a brief furlough from the dusty bookshelf; temporarily leaving a conspicuous gap between its other out-of- print human potential neighbors. Its return to life was inspired by a visit to the Ashley. Not only for its reference to dance, but for the characters. Odd characters, I thought to be forever consigned to the yellowed and cockroach nibbled pages of a forgotten past. Apparently, these odd characters have been freed from the dog-eared printed page, and found new life. Returning like a Lazarus looking like Keith Richard's dressed in a lime-green leisure suit. Take David Morgan for example...

    David is one of my competitors in the mental health business. You may know us better as head shrinkers. Technically speaking, we don't shrink heads anymore, because the psychoanalytic couch trip has become passé. The final bastions of the couch trip are the White House where presidential interns are interviewed for sensitive government positions and at Water Bed City show rooms where customers are allowed to comfort test the inventory and discuss their sleep hygiene with a concerned salesperson. David and I just talk to people and don't do any cozy couch sessions for fear of a malpractice suit. Poor David was diagnosed last year with kidney disease. He was placed on the organ donor list for a kidney. Unfortunately he began to experience kidney failure before a donor match was found. Fortunately, David was blessed with the luck of the Irish. His benevolent vagabond lass of a sister returned from her world travels in the nick of time; was found to be a donor match and so gave up a kidney of her own to save her brother's arse. Ever since the operation David has well, to put it delicately, *changed*. Change that's different from the therapeutic kinds of change we're used to seeing in patients. I'm not talking here about developing a 'brighter affect', 'engaging in more positive self-talk' or abstaining from using mood altering substances. I mean David has experienced this...transformation. Before the operation, David was the mildest and most conservative guy you'd ever want to meet. He presented as the well-grounded, Rational-Emotive therapist who, at least in public, never fought, cursed or drank. In fact it was rumored that he had had his Irish demons exorcized many years ago and had been on the wagon and on the straight and narrow ever since. That is, until the kidney operation. Blame it on the Ashley or on the fact that it was a girl kidney that he got. Regardless, David was bewitched. Eve, whose theories about these things are rarely as erudite as mine, thinks it had more to do with the kidney. To which she added, "You know, Stewart, people who have received donor organs have been known to take on the personality traits of their donors. It's unusual, but there are rare, reported cases of this sort of thing happening. Maybe it's a genetic memory transfer. No one really understands how it happens. A Harvard research group is investigating it." "You mean David might not be *just* David now that his sister's genes have co-mingled with his own?" " No, Stewart, it's not as dramatic as that. They're usually subtle changes. Like cravings for foods the recipient never ate or even liked before, or a shift in a preference like music or such." "But, Eve, have you seen David lately?" "Yes, of course I have, Stewart. We see him at the Ashley all the time." "And?" "And, what, Stewart?" "Get to the point ." Eve, always the one to limit her theories to mere research studies. And to rely on the findings of a Harvard study team that's never been to the Ashley. So, as diplomatically as I could put it, said, "God damn it, Eve, the fucking guy's whacked!" "Look. See, the resemblance, to Lorie, his wild Irish sister?" "Stewart, I never met Lorie. How would I see a resemblance if I've never met her?" "Eve, when have you ever known David to down a fifth of Bushmills, and sing a soprano dedication to his sister in a voice as sweet and melancholy as the lead singer of the Cranberries?" "We were all partying that night to celebrate St. Patrick's Day." "And where was his bonnie wife, Deidre, that night?" "And who was that *guy* on whose knee his hand was resting - a wee bit too long, I might add?" "Oh, Stewart, you read too much into things. I heard that he and Deidre are getting a divorce. Poor guy was probably just feeling lonely." "Yeah, that's for sure." "And why did you say it that way?" "Because when you left to go to the ladies room with Nancy, David asked me to dance."

    David sans Deidre continues to frequent the Ashley. He's seen regularly in the company of friends with whom he goes fishing in Key West a lot. Eve commented that he has a beautiful tan, and seems much happier now. Frankly I'm a little suspicious about those fishing trips. When I asked him whether he trolled or bottom fished, he put his hand over his mouth and giggled. He never did answer the question. We are still on friendly terms. I think it's great that he's gotten in touch with his sister's feminine side. And David respects that I'm a wall flower. He doesn't ask me to dance anymore...and I don't ask him about his fishing trips anymore.

You're probably convinced by now that this isn't a manual on dance, an encyclopedia of Florida birds, or a fishing guide. No. It is none of these. It's about the Ashley, a one of a kind place where like the call to priesthood; many are called, yet few are chosen. How are the few selected? What admissions tests or initiation must they pass to enter this fraternity? As far as I can figure - after being pulled into the orbit of the Ashley, and docked at its threshold - you can pay the bouncer the five-dollar cover charge, pop the hatch and walk on in. To obtain pedigree, the sincere adherent to the bhikku brotherhood can see Madame Jacqueline for a tarot reading. And on the basis of a favorable interpretation of the arcana, you can find out if you are worthy to be counted among the bar Bodhisattvas. For Madame Jacqueline...*knows*. Knows, because she *sees* your worthiness through her Celtic gift of second sight - and also by your performance on the dance floor – that you are a big, wiggly keeper among all of those big fish dredged from the pool of humanity. A sorting process that for Madame Jacqueline can be compared with separating manatees from mullet. Her second sight should be tested for astigmatism (now I'm sounding skeptical like Eve). I say this because of a reading Eve got from the Ashley oracle. What happened was that Eve, instead of getting *her* reading from Madame Jackie, got someone else's. And that someone else was..well, I think, me. Maybe it was because she was using the none-too-accurate Royal Fez Moroccan tarot deck. I've talked to some people from the Unity Church since it happened, and they told me that they wouldn't rely on the Royal Fez Moroccan spread if their reincarnated lives depended upon it.

Cecil, an expert on the arcana, and former Las Vegas black jack dealer, told me that that particular deck had the accuracy of a Shriner taking a drunken aim at the urinal. Maybe Madame Jacqueline lost her clairvoyant aim that evening. Her psychic cross-hairs might have been off the mark (so to speak). Eve was really disappointed because she was in the mood for a reading. In fact she needed one. You see, every few months Eve gets the urge to prime her destiny with a reading. For her it's affirming, and a reading helps her reset her compass when she encounters the occasional fork in the road and doesn't know which way to turn. As for myself, I avoid psychics and fortune tellers. I much prefer sticking to Tennyson's guidance about mastering one's own destiny. Even if it is with the crude navigational device of my own wit. Eve says it's my business if I want to negotiate the hazards of life wearing a blindfold. She was on a roll that evening tossing a metaphor here and a maxim there; finally assuming a smugness that teed me off. "A tarot reading represents a pin-hole in the blindfold", and that she would rather navigate life's potential pitfalls with any available advantage. And, furthermore, it was my macho inflated pride that kept me from asking Madame Jacqueline for a blindfold with a pin-hole in it. Eve was offended by me distorting her analogy. What she called "corrupting a perfectly apt metaphor." That was because I remarked, "A condom with the same defect is a liability. And that the future influenced by either having a pin-hole could be disastrous. Most people who would rather leave their destiny to a higher power, and a paid up life insurance policy." Even if that higher power had a warped sense of humor. Bottom line...I was willing to take my chances with my eyes open. And if she dared me, I'd walk home blindfolded, as long as she didn't deliberately steer me into traffic. My smug expression was a premature claim to victory over Eve who's conceded on many an occasion that she is no match for my verbal chicanery. Her definition for that: is that I cheat when we argue because I have a way with words that Webster never intended. A kick in the groin would have been kinder than Eve's ultimate foul. She sucker punched me when she brought up, within earshot of strangers, that I, Stewart the Cognitive-Behavioral psychologist was a closet Jungian.

And that I had, secreted away in my dresser drawer, under my socks and underwear, a well-worn deck of Thoth tarot cards designed by the devil-man himself, Aleister Crowley. "Foul!" I cried. "They're just a curiosity. They help me better relate to my superstitious patients, and to those poor Satanic cult survivors." "But, Stewart, I've heard you give such...insightful readings. Remember when you gave Carol the reading, and you told her that she was pregnant before she had the courage to announce it?" "That was just a lucky guess, considering Carol had gained thirty pounds, and her belly stuck out like a beach ball. And, besides her *subtle* weight gain and shape, she was drinking pickle juice out of the Claussens jar which she'd helped herself to from our refrigerator." "Oh, Stewart, you're too humble to admit that you have the gift of *seeing*, like your Welsh mother." Bringing my mother into it was the lowest that Eve had stooped in hours.

And what of the tarot reading intended for Eve? Actually, I was its target. Can you believe it? It astounds me what had happened: I was *read* from across the room by the Helen Keller of tarot card readers.

Madame Jackie is seated at a card table between the front door and the bar. She is a pre-Raphaelite figure of a woman. The kind of woman that skinny, bald men wearing saffron robes bow to. A woman-kind figure that inspires respect rather than adoration. Maybe even fear for her witchy ways, and for her knowing about what lies hidden in a stranger's troubled heart. This is the image of the Madame Jackie with whom Eve anticipated becoming acquainted that evening. What I imagined was that this was a cat lady, whose house contained a dozen cats and as many litter boxes. And the prospect of such a meeting didn't excite me. No disrespect to the oracle of the Ashley, but it was cat contact of any sort that I sought to avoid. It just so happens that I'm allergic to the fortune tellers' feline familiars. And because of the noticeable patches of cat hair on Madame Jackie' Italian Renaissance dress, in whose big pockets I imagined a litter of kittens lay cuddled, I decided to give her a wide berth. Eve approached Madame Jackie for a reading while I side shuffled off seeking to blend with the Ashley's Lascaux horse murals, colorful patrons, and hovering angels. I chose a near-by column, to lean against. Safely located, I thought, outside the sneeze and watery eyes range of Madame J's thick dander. It wasn't the Madame's cat dander that leapt the gap. It was her Sandy Duncan inability to focus her gaze in a straight line. Her third eye wanders I suspect. If it were the average eyeball, you would call it a lazy eye. She should have concentrated more on making eye contact with Eve. And she should have known that a reading beginning with: "You're a man who can't keep his hands off his wife, and his eyes off of others," didn't belong to Eve. At first this utterance didn't faze Madame J, who's obviously accustomed to the novelty and diversity of the Ashley crowd, and who probably read the 1978 Ballantine edition of *The Dance Away Lover*.

It was Eve's, "Whaaaht the fu_ _", and her hateful glance in my direction that got the Madame's attention...and *grabbed* mine. Madame Jackie was taken aback, and attempted to regain her composure by apologizing for the "miss", and blaming the error on sunspot activity. I saw her close her eyes, and bring the next card to her forehead. After a moment of communing with a trump card of the Royal Fez, she said (loud enough for me to hear her six feet away over the din of the crowd), "You work in a profession that involves healing. You are very good at what you do. People respond well to your touch." So far, so good. Eve was being read like a billboard...until Madame J opened her eyes, and continued... "I see you working with an unscrupulous man. He wants what you have to offer. Yet he wants you for nothing. He is ill-dignified in his purpose for he only pretends to offer you your true worth. Beware...it is his intention to expose your assets, and exploit them to satisfy his selfish desires. Beware of his treachery. At first you are attracted to this man whose characteristics are seduction, secret violence and the craft of artifice." I, imagining a swarthy stranger, no a satyr, being stroked with pink emu feathers by a smitten Eve. "You are burning with desire for what he has to offer. His offer is large." Oh yeah? I think to myself. How large? These fortune tellers are never really specific. And I feel my blood begin to heat, because I'm trying to figure this out, you know ...competitively. "He is an artist of deceit whose sober exterior masks a seething passion, caring intensely for power and relentless in his aim to possess you."

Well, Madame Jackie must have switched to the Xavier Hollander tarot deck without us noticing. Or my devoted wife Eve was living a secret life right out of the pages of a Jackie Collins novel, and was carrying on with Fabian the satyr who was also a bouncer at the Ashley. Eve had the nerve to pipe up defensively, "Look Lady, I know it's not me you're reading, but I think I can guess who's 'R' rated future you may have channel surfed onto. Stewart! This is your reading isn't it?"

As if I, wearing a blindfold without a pin hole in it, could provide seeing-eye-dog assistance to Madame Jackie. Perhaps I *had* inherited my Welsh mother's gift of second sight, or - I happened to recall - that George Goffman, the Mediwell Managed Care mogul, had approached me last month and expressed an interest in buying my private practice. It was my recollection of the recent business dealing that struck the gong of recognition. Suddenly realizing that Madame Jackie had read my business and not Eve's. Thank goodness! I felt obligated to help restore Madame Jackie's dignity and defend Eve's chastity in a protective, chauvinistic out-moded fashion. So, I modestly offered a saving interpretation. "Hey, you must have picked up my super strong vibes. I've been tested by Duke University parapsychologists, and I test out as a natural born telepathic 'sender'. My thoughts can be read a mile away by a super-sensitive "receiver" like you. So don't feel bad. You couldn't have known that you were picking up on a business transaction I've been involved with. And gee, thanks for the warning. I knew there was something about George that couldn't be trusted."

    Eve should have been consoled by such a deft save. So I don't know why she decided to hang onto what felt like uh…negative vibes for the rest of the evening. I suggested to Eve that she, too, might be hypersensitive to dander which would account for her flushed complexion. Even Madame Jackie tried to smooth over the damage she had nearly done to Eve's moral character by offering her money back. Eve declined, not wanting poor Madame J to suffer any further embarrassment for having accidentally homed in on the confidential business of Stewart, the Welsh Mother's Seventh Son of a Seventh Son. I insisted that Eve accept the refund. Eve's neck stiffened so you could see the cabled muscles that look like the ones connecting suspension bridges. Then her nostrils flared in the cutest way just before she told me in the leveled voice of a sociopath about to take his oral bar exam, "You got what I paid for, so drop it." To Madame Jacqueline I suggested switching to the Gong Hee Fot Choy deck…in the original Mandarin Chinese. The same advanced race that invented gun powder, mahjong, and eye glasses.

"Before you see a lawyer, read <u>The Dance Away lover.</u>" - Ann Landers

I have no idea what Ann Landers intended by that remark. After having read the book, and in it discovering my ex-wife and me between its covers, it refuted Anne's advice; confirmed my belief that my ex had done the right thing. She filed for divorce that same year. It was the best thing she could have done for the both of us. I snared Nancy after a long courtship, and pinned her to the mounting board of legal matrimony. It took a long time before I began experiencing her emotional chilliness toward me as the ultimate form of feminist sabotage. She, 'the most likely to exceed Ayn Rand' (read her college yearbook entry) revealed, behind that porcelain exterior of hers, a will of purest iron. This relationship can be compared to a racing greyhound catching 'Rusty', the mechanical rabbit. You can imagine the dog's – and my - disappointment.

"THE ANCIENT POETS tell us that Venus, the goddess of love, was born in a chill and effortless moment of self-procreation from the foam of the surging sea. Poets also tell us that she took as her most illustrious lover, Mars, the god of strife."

    From, <u>The Dance Away Lover</u>
      By, Daniel Goldstine, Katherine Larner, Shirley Zuckerman & Hilary Goldstine

Such classic and ill-fated love relationships have been constant throughout the ages. However, their frequency has increased over the last half century. The Ashley couples are no exception. In fact, their numbers exceed those of the general population's. Only the love-lorne who haunt the singles' bars live greater tragic lives. This is why the Ashley attracts so many patrons from among the helping professions. We drink and socialize there in the spirit of professional over-time. We are truth be told, to drum up business; to help either reconcile the relationships of people who have a fighting chance, or help facilitate the separation of the ones who shouldn't have paired up in the first place. The bar tenders account very little for the chemical attraction that people seem to have for one another in this most unusual attraction between social opposites. The espousers of the 'love conquers all' philosophy have seen successes where the laws of nature forbid such unions, and where states have civil and criminal laws which do the same.

Some of the most unlikely individuals have coupled up at the Ashley on those weekends of mingling, mating and dance. Like Darla Albetti, and Doug Blake...and Darla Albetti and Jeff Straight...and Darla Albetti and Bryce McCrery. It can be said of Darla that she is looking for Mr. Anyguy in all the team locker rooms. And Mr. Right – this week - in the No.1 jersey is bound and gagged and imprisoned in Darla's imaginary tall metal locker. Only she can hear the muffled sound of her named being called through the fluted air vents in the door. "Darla, I'm in here honey. Please let me out. I'll dance with you if you do." Darla is the only one hearing the voice. Eve says everyone keeps a running dialogue going in their head. She accuses me of having my own demons. Fortunately, they don't interrupt me with their strange ideas when I'm trying to think. As for Darla, she feels less alone among the angels of the Ashley, then among its patrons. Eve avoids her; veering from her approach like an Aikido master. I don't mind Darla's overtures of psychedelic friendliness. I think of her as a sixties break from the boorish Mac-In Crowd. Eve had to admit that Darla is the bar's premier rubberneck attraction. An I-95 roll-over accident comes in second to an entrance by Darla.

"THE ANXIOUS INGENUE

She offers herself on free trial, no strings attached, and then wonders why there are so many returns..."

From, <u>The dance Away Lover</u>
By, Daniel Goldstine, Katherine Larner, Shirley Zuckerman & Hilary Goldstine

When Darla enters the bar your ears pop from the vacuum her presence creates. She absorbs all of the shadow, the sound and the exhaled breath of everyone in the room. She is virtually a creature of the night, whose bone china sheen is an undertaker's art. Eve said that I'm imposing a gothic chic by describing her complexion that way. She maintains that Darla is merely just heavy handed with the oil of ole and the lip gloss. And that her chalky-white paleness is due to an aversion to the sun. "Maybe she has xeroderma pigmentosa. Or maybe she works like the rest of us natives, and never gets to sunbathe as often as the tourists." To which I add, "Maybe she's a Kabuki actress, or...maybe she's dead, and is an unhappy spirit cursed to visit the Ashley every Friday night till she finds a partner that can dance. " "Well then, Stewart, stay away from her, or the poor soul will never find peace."

  Be she dead or alive Darla is striking. Morbid, but striking. And very unusual. She has a preference for wearing black dresses. Simple, yet elegant apparel (this is David Morgan talking), into which she has zipped the body of Olive Oyle. The contrast of black fabric on white skin is stunning. If Darla were a yogi and could do the sasangasana rabbit pose she'd be a dead ringer for the yin-yang symbol familiar to the bar Bodhisattvas. Not to mention being a show stopper for demonstrating the flexible skill of a contortionist...in a short dress.

  Darla is liquid night. Her presence tones down the brightness of this well-lighted place. She moves through a corridor of shadow into which the men given her attention step blindly. Most likely fascinated by her dark, etheric countenance. Like unwitting prey caught in the web of a she spider with an appetite for mating followed by murder. Since I'm a trained clinician I'm immune to her evil charms - this is how I explain my interest in her to Eve. I detect a draft of cold air when she comes near. I asked Eve if she ecognized the perfume Darla wore. Eve's guess was "Poison" by Elizabeth Taylor (Eve, I suspected was sharing my gothic chic theme). I can't place a fragrance like Al Pacino could in "The Scent of a Woman." Especially one that stung the wasabi regions of my sinuses after breathing in her vapor. Eve attributed this to male olfactory numbness, and then jabbed with bringing up the three grams of cocaine I snorted in 1978 thinking it was mint snuff. Well, I think Darla carries the smell of death. I know it's morbid. So read Kubler-Ross to help you get past it. Al would have guessed that the scent of this woman was the fragrance of Easter lilies laced with formaldehyde.

It isn't as though Darla were always a drooling spirit. I knew her when she was ...more alive. I can't say that I knew her all that well. Eve and I met Darla through our daughter, Angie, who was a classmate of Darla's daughter, Jennifer. In fact, once upon a time Darla was the iconic 'homemaker' of the fifties. Or rather, Darla learned the part and acted it out on the stage called life. Darla played the part like Nancy Cunningham did on 'Happy Days.' That doting mother to Richie and Maggie, and the proper 50's wife of Arnold Cunningham. In real life, Darla came closer to playing understudy to Morticia Adams. And her real life Gomez was a nefarious salesman whose line of work required that he travel a lot. Gomez, a.k.a., Ben Albetti, made a reasonably good living organizing home and garden shows throughout the Southern United States. He was particularly attracted to those Avon sun dress models who distribute helium balloons, candies and Asti Spumoni to convention goers. You know the kind of girl from whom Al would have picked up the scent of "Youth Dew", fresh strawberries and cream. Girls masquerading as wholesome Nancy homemakers, whose freckles, silicon breasts and Brazilian butt lifts would drive Ben to distraction. It was this composite material of space age, durable beauty - a mixture of helium-Asti-silicon-and re-distributed fat - that made Ben board the Tantric Tours company bus and leave the comparatively drab and dreary Darla. You can say that Darla is better off without her Gomez, but she loved her Home Show Lothario in spite of his minor character defects. She was devastated by the loss. Eve calls her a fool for pining the loss of, 'the jerk whose little head ruled his life and ruined hers.' She said nothing to me this time, because my bigger head told me to keep my mouth shut and my comments to myself.

Darla and her brood never even came close to being the idealized T.V. family. The Albettis were their own reality show. Her little Pugsly, a.k.a., Benji, was a pint size free spirit who Darla allowed to express himself at an early age. Perhaps she should have kept him locked in the closet, or at least bound in the attic with one hand free to play Nintendo. Maybe, just maybe, Benji might have had a chance at being normal. Instead, Darla took Benji out and about with her; *he* clad in *her* underwear. She acted as if this were a perfectly normal expression of childhood dress up. She should have at least told him to wear the brassier under the slip, and that the care instruction tag on the panties goes in the back. Poor Benji was all of five years old when he was allowed to shop at Victoria's Secret instead of Toys 'R' Us. I judge the Albettis not. After all Ben had recently abandoned his family, and Darla and the children were upset by the loss. I would be glad to have them as patients.

As the saying goes, if it weren't for bad luck, some people wouldn't have any luck at all. This is true for Darla. It probably explains her departure from a reality that was already fragile and tenuous at best. Life can be difficult for everyone.

It was after my daughter, Angie's, visit with Jennifer at the Albetti mausoleum, that I forbade any further visits. I refer to it as a 'mausoleum because of the dead animals that were left to decompose beneath the Albettis living room sofa. Darla showed them to Eve when she arrived to pick up Angie. If Darla were a Santeria holy woman I'd have understood her need to collect dead animals. As it were, Darla had left the still-born dead puppy litter that Reba, the family dog, had deposited there the week before. Eve was trying to be understanding and sympathetic about Darla's explanation that she hadn't removed the dead puppies because she didn't want to upset Reba or the children by dragging the lifeless puppies from beneath the sofa. It must have gotten harder to pretend that the puppies were sleeping as week two approached. Eve gently recommended immediate internment and a rug shampoo.

If memory doesn't fail, it was no more than a week that had passed when we heard the Channel 12 news anchorman report that the house at 52 Bougainvillea Lane had burned to the ground in an early morning blaze. The house was that belonging to the Albettis. The news anchorman reported in the solemn tone and arched eyebrows of practiced empathy: "An early morning blaze today destroyed the home of a single mother and her family; leaving them homeless and without food or clothing. It is believed that the fire may have been caused by a frayed electrical cord beneath the carpet in the living room. Everything Ms. Albetti and her children owned was destroyed in the fire. Our live action cam shows a Red Cross volunteer escorting the family to a local hotel where they will be given temporary shelter. The volunteer spokeswoman told our action cam reporter that no one was injured in the blaze. The little boy clutching his mother's hand, and sobbing deeply said to her, 'the puppies are now in heaven with Jesus.' We can only conclude at this time that the family's pets died in the fire. Fortunately, no one else was injured." Eve and I looked at one another without a word. It was Eve who broke the silence. Her incredulity giving way to *knowing* with the dry comment, "I guess Darla decided on a cremation."

We didn't see Darla or learn of her fate after that funeral fire. Not until her resurrection at the Ashley more than a year later. Her sudden appearance only enhanced her mystique. Here she was, the mythical phoenix; having risen from the ashes of that house fire...to make her debut at the Ashley.

> Ashes to Ashley,
> Sundown to dusk,
> Darla's a vampire,
> and Eve says *I'm* nuts.

Yet Eve will tell you that she has never run into Darla anywhere during the day. Not even at the Publix Supermarket. Now everybody shops for groceries. Why doesn't Darla? Eve, who even having read two of Anne Rice's books, said that it was probably because she shopped at the all-night Walmart. Well I've been there more than a few times and I haven't seen her there. My theory stands unchallenged. There has not yet been a reported day-time sighting of Darla - the 'Bride of Dracula,' and patron of the Ashley after dark.

The patrons of the Ashley arrive two-by-two, singly, manage-a-tois and folie-a-deux, and in assortments never before seen. Julian Barnes', in his entertaining, nay enlightening, revisionist account of Noah's ark in, *A History of the World in 10 ½ Chapters,* supports my theory regarding the *true purpose* of the Ashley. It is the new ark (not Newark). It is, as I've pointed out, at the event horizon of Confusion Corner; around and through which the manifest pass. Not all are chosen to experience the voyage. The selection process is a clever one accommodated by the owners. They are most certainly the modern Mr. and Ms. Moses - whose net link to the Almighty would surprise the established religious authority of our day. Their methods will soon be explained.

   I casually ran this idea about Dodge's ark by Jack Dudlos. He's the former Bible salesman, who I consider to be a learned man of the Word. Jack has a Divinity Degree which is why his closest friends call him 'Reverend Jack.' His detractors (certainly not regulars of the bar) say his credentials are bogus because they say he got his degree through a shady correspondence program during the Viet Nam era. They have the nerve to accuse him of having tried to evade the Selective Service's lottery with the popular minister-of-a-flock ruse. Jack has it on the record that before that mess in Southeast Asia really heated up after the Tet Offensive that he had volunteered to serve as an Army chaplain at Hingham Airfield in Hawaii, the site of infamy which took place, December 7, 1941. Jack doesn't have to defend himself to me. I didn't know Jack back then. I was vacationing at a friend's duck farm in Ontario. At least Jack had the courage volunteer to put on the uniform. What is impressive is that Jack knows his product. His talent for quoting chapter and verse rivals that of the 700 Club's best. And Jack possesses humility to boot. Jack, like his competitors in the T.V. evangelism business, made a modest fortune, if not as many actual converts.

   I trust Jack's intuition about these post- millennium times in which we live. And when I proposed the Ashley-is-the-Ark theory to Jack, he said that my idea certainly had merit if not Vatican endorsement. And that it warranted serious study by the Jesuits. He said I not only had the makings of an excellent telepathic sender, but the visionary perspicacity of a prophet. Jack is pretty psychic. He guessed that I, like him, had experienced the permanently lasting religious ecstasy caused by a few acid trips during the 60s. He even let me express my gratitude by accepting another drink I insisted on buying him. I watched Reverend Jack down it like a thirsting prophet. And by the third round of Christian Brother's brandy, our apostolate became solidified. And without the imprimatur of Rome, or the scholarship of the Jesuits. Though Eve's agnostic cynicism didn't dissolved at the bar-of-the-ark as I had hoped it might. She looked me dead in the eye and said in all seriousness, "And why would a middle aged man like you with an irreversible vasectomy, be chosen to board an ark? Stewart, remember your Bible school education; two-by-two they entered the ark. You know the reasoning behind the two-for-one cruise tickets?" "Well, Eve, it's obviously not that kind of ark. Think of it as...as a gathering place for a group who defy the ordinary. Whose originality is that they lack sameness. A group just as diverse as the ark passengers; only these will be the architects of social change, not the 'chosen' of God's planned parenthood committee. You're interpreting the idea too literally. And besides I think they can reverse those vasectomies now." When I looked down after focusing on the Angel above the bar, not wanting to meet Eve's disapproving glare until I was ready, I was surprised to see her holding her head in her hands. She was doing something that sounded like low murmuring. I couldn't make out what she was saying. I figured she was either agreeing with me, or she was saying her prayers. I shouldn't have interrupted Eve's introspective silence, but I couldn't help myself. "You know Eve; the distance from Confusion Corner to the ass end of the Ashley is three hundred cubits. Did you know that?" "I'm afraid to ask, Stewart. So what is the significance of your chariot's odometer reading?" "Eve, three hundred cubits was the length of Noah's ark."

This ark theory pertaining to the Ashley is plausible in my thinking, albeit based on an ancient biblical legend. The original ark tale does have a basis in fact. However, like most of the history available to us today, it has been revised and either reviles or acquits the deeds of our ancestors. Face it Christian fundamentalists, the Book of Genesis, The Flood, Noah's ark; it was all a cover story for a *God's honest mistake* (of global proportions), and of a man who had the good sense to take refuge in his house boat when the Good Lord left the faucet running in the Israelites' part of the world. Maybe it happened while He was tending greener pasture somewhere else on the planet. Being the all-knowing God that He is, He realized that He'd really screwed up. He was gone for the entire year instead of the season, and when He got back to Middle East, He found His house flooded. At first He must have been upset, and then relieved that there were no witnesses to His having drowned the kittens, so to speak. Imagine His surprise when He sees Noah's ark bobbing like a cork around his sandals as he sloshed through Israel, like a kid running through a puddle after a storm. It was then I suspect that God "created" an explanation for His accidental drowning of a million Assyrians, Babylonians and Hebrews. He told a water-soaked and wrinkled Noah that He had brought the Deluge upon the people as a punishment for their misbehavior. And that He was indeed glad that He had spared Noah and His family because they were *just*, and a lot smarter than most for having gotten out of the rain, and into something that could stay afloat until He got back. Noah bought the story hook, line and sinker. He was glad to have the place to himself. Well not all by himself. Because Noah's son, Ham, had been responsible for seating the stand-bys after the family and pets were safely ensconced aboard the ark. Ham had invited a hundred Babylonian women and situated them aboard his brother's sloop for the Hurricane party. Noah remained a happy man until his death at the ripe of nine hundred and fifty. God was delighted to have Noah around to spread the word of the benevolent Lord. God had Noah edit the ship's log, and called it Genesis 6-9.   Modern attempts to borrow from the example of Genesis water stories haven't been as successful; such as with Watergate, or the White Water deal.

Julian Barnes knew what he was talking about when he speculated that the ark was not just one ark. He concluded that the ark, as it were, consisted of a flotilla of eight vessels. To Julian, the eighth vessel represents a mystery of sorts. For me it holds the key to the salvation of the species. A lost, but recently discovered supra-species - that is now gathering for its reunion at the Ashley.

Julian describes the eighth vessel as:
"...a darting little sloop with filigree decorations in sandalwood all along the stern, it steered a course sycophantically close to that of Ham's ark. If you got to leeward you would sometimes be teased with strange perfumes; occasionally, at night, when the tempest slackened, you could hear jaunty music and shrill laughter - surprising noises to us, because we had assumed that all the wives of all the sons of Noah were safely ensconced on their own ships. However, this scented, laughing boat was not robust: it went down in a sudden squall, and Ham was pensive for several weeks thereafter.

From: <u>A History of the World in 10 ½ Chapters</u>
By: Julian Barnes

Maybe Julian mistakenly thought the sloop to have sunk. This is clearly a case of error-by-commission. As I see it, that sloop didn't sink. It may have been missing from the radar screen and presumed lost: an intentionally contrived lost-at-sea report. I believe master-minded by none other than father and son. Noah and Ham were in cahoots, because they had already gotten a raft of complaints from their wives. Wives suspicious, ugly (not stupid) and curious about that spritely little sloop with its pretty smelling and vocally musical cargo. How were Noah and Ham to explain to their wives that God had commanded them to gather the finest species of women on earth, "the fairest in all the land"; to save them from drowning in the flood, and for future propagation.

And that they, the wives of Noah and Ham didn't satisfy the definition of "fair". And why didn't God nix this whole business after he found out about the scheme? Are you kidding? After what God had done. He was more than willing to settle quid pro quo with Noah for graciously accepting His apology for the Flood mistake.

Truth be known, there were other passengers who stowed aboard the sloop. They were - how to put it delicately - fair men; who's beauty, too, out-shown the Noah family females (even though the wildebeests aboard were prettier than them). And they weighed a damned sight less too. But the boys, as they were, were pretty boys, given to frivolous mischief and buck, ass-naked horsing around (if you know what I mean) with Ham's brother, Janus, who delighted in their company (if you know what I mean). Okay, so they were gay. And much like it is now, it was tolerated and accepted as a form of ancient birth control, and as a source of bouncers willing to dress like women to re-enact bank robberies. Anyway, Ham was happy with the arrangement, and that is why Ham put Janus in charge of his and pop's 'precious cargo.'

That sloop is important to the colonization of the world after the Flood. Had it not been for its special passengers, the world would be an awfully boring place (like Texas). Think. Imagine a world of two-fors, pre-sorted, packaged-in-pairs animals and people. The original ark majority is easy to pick out of the general population. They're the ones who start going steady at twelve, marry their high school sweethearts, wear power ties, do lunch and work for the government. The sloop generation? Now they defy classification. They prefer to remain single or divorce often, have more than two drinks, and either remains unemployed or work in unusual occupations. And they sure as hell can't dance. How can something so basic, to start with, be so difficult? Something requiring a partner and simple two-step locomotion. Yet, this is the crowd who shows up at Ashley.

It's precisely why the world is in crisis. We can hope that the descendants of the sloop passengers will redeem them. Hallelujah! It is the mission of the sloop people to bring the rank and file out of their vertically oriented bondage. They do not want to go from a lost to a vanishing tribe. It is when only in significant in the numbers that a species can ensure its survival. And according to the leading authorities of evolutionary psychology, it is critical that the strong –who can dance – help those who can't. There is nothing more frightening to a 1375th generation Deluge survivor than becoming fused into a global world and popped out of a cookie cutter education system destined to live a Mr. and Mrs. Gingerbread life. Those fatuous ninnies happy to live in a condo or a walled community. Nothing is more frightening than conforming to the norms of pairing. Well, except a terrible thunder storm and a lot of rain.

Sunshine or rain, the bar is a port in the storm for everyday stress. It's a welcomed escape from the mainstream for the wandering herds. Its importance rivals St. Augustine's Fountain of Youth, and Versace's South Beach mansion. Landmarks with which the Ashley shares many things in common. Like the Bodhisattva's search for eternal youth, and the refreshing rush (or debt) of oxygenated blood; induced by excessive drinking, acting young and foolish, and dancing close to Darla. There is a real fusion of energies in the Ashley's exogamous cultural potpourri. This well-lighted place is a beacon showing the way to the port-of-call and pre-Rapture gathering platform for the ark's descendants. The descendants arrive in conveyances and costumes of every description. And for each arrival it is a debut. Every hit-or-trip entrance, approximation of conversation, and attempt at dance is an audition. The audition is the modality through which the Sons and Daughters of the Society of the Eighth Ark identify the needy. I wish them God speed, and a better sense of direction and navigation than was the pace, luck and skill of the original Moses group. Noah's ark, as you may recall, ended up high and dry on a mountain top in Turkey. Janus' sloop ended up a few leagues behind on what was later to become the site of the Turkish prison on which the movie, "The Midnight Express" was based. It is believed that the real-life prison superintendent was a direct descendant of Bubals, Janus' first mate and best buddy. The rest of the crew had little regret about leaving Bubals behind. They soon got fed up with his rough housing, and his aggressiveness when practicing 'Brotherly Love'. So they left him behind and, with Janus in tears, they walked back to Israel with the remainder of their shipwrecked party. The prettiest of the female cargo could only make it as far as Italy and France. And it was in these far-flung, fertile lands that they chose to settle. The hardier and more muscular of the pretties were able to trek farther into the regions of the North and East. All of them set about to do the work that the Lord had intended, and they multiplied abundantly and enthusiastically. Some of those who made up the original ark manifest regarded the job of repopulating the earth as a chore. Nonetheless they complied, or else such places where women still wear kerchiefs and wool pantyhose and all look like the Queen Mother would remain unpopulated to this day.

And the modern day audition that I was describing? Well open the doors and let the curtain rise. And…let the band begin.

CHAPTER 8

..."auditions!!"

As a Baby Boomer, I'm ashamed for not having passed on the wisdom of the 60s to our succeeding generation. Now here it is only – who knows – maybe months away from the end of the Mayan calendar or the cataclysmic meteor impact that will incinerate the earth, and again wipe out the dinosaur - this time the Homo sapiens dinosaur. And what have I done about it? What *can* I still contribute to our slim chance for survival, other than the same old Happy Global Village social speak, and something else more 'Green' to eat or convert. Not another televangelist buy-a-prayer-to-save-your-ass campaign, or another episode of 'Survivor.' If PBS airs 'Prophesies of Nostradamus' again this season I'll vomit pea soup.

What could I offer that would make the slightest difference? Saving the endangered and arguably un-advanced homo simian from imminent extinction is an awesome responsibility. And frankly I believe it's a job better left to chance, social apathy, and the timely intervention of the Eighth Ark descendants; henceforth understood to be to those who can dance, and can teach others to do the same. Because there is real shame in not being able to dance to the Top Ten and the Golden Oldies. Or to keep your feet moving to the rhythms of the contemporary beat. The Ashley dancers know - yes, know, Hallelujah! - That it ain't a comet that's gonna get ya. No siree, it's the 6 o'clock news, and imitating fashion and entertainment that's gonna do y'all in. They know that ultimately it will be the fierce undertow of the swift moving mainstream that's gonna suck us down and drown us. Just like happened before in the Big Flood. Eve hasn't commented on any of this, because she knows there's no point in arguing with someone whom she left off saying, "you're trying to revise the work of John Calvin as if he'd dropped acid." Well, I can assure you, if not Eve, that I don't mean this in a Southern Baptist don't-have-any-fun, always wear a bra or boxers shorts sort of way. The Ashley patrons provide the better example for a winnable argument. The antipathy of out-moded religious and social constructs *is* what the Ashley patron represents. These crazy rock'n, bebop'n dervishes look like the Poconos guests in 'Dirty Dancing.' You know they need a fix. Take Harold for example...

    Harold Frognath is a friend of mine. When he isn't running the Sociology Department at the local state college he's espousing social theory at the Ashley. He does this gratuitously as a free seminar to anyone willing to listen; much like he did during the 60's when he was a graduate student at Columbia. Back then his followers were in awe, but in an altered consciousness sort of way. Harold knew better than to quiz them on the material. He was happy to hear a "WOW" every so often from the stoned out gatherings. He really felt appreciated, he told me, when a Goldie Hawn look-alike flower child made him her guru. Now Harold is satisfied with his tenure and his Cass Elliott. His celebrated theories, found in his published articles on 'The Times in Which We Live,' have enjoyed a renaissance at the Ashley.

Harold cornered Eve and I one evening in a booth from which we couldn't easily escape and educated us about the year 2012 being the end of a cycle from which a new era is about to begin. Talk about Stuart being the epicenter of change! And right here in this same small town is this guy who's reporting it live from this downtown Mobius strip of socio-genetic re-engineering, and the advent of newly evolving dance forms. According to Harold, *here* is the culture that will instigate great changes that we'll get to witness with our own eyes. To me, Harold Frognath is the Dick Clark of the Ashley. Eve says that Harold and I share a similar world view, and that if it doesn't change soon she's preparing the Kool Aid in the unlikely event that Harold and I should actually begin attracting any followers. I told Eve that I preferred my guarded optimism and less sugary drinks to her hostile, feminist, post-modern pessimism. I made the faut pas of extrapolating, with Harold's needling encouragement, that her not so thinly disguised mean tempered disagreement was not unlike that smiling Kool Aid pitcher logo in which lurked the lethal dose of strychnine. Eve bought Harold and me the next round of drinks. She brought them to the table herself and offered them so cheerfully. I was afraid to drink mine. She seemed disappointed that I never touched it. She added upon leaving that evening, "Stewart, aren't you going to finish your drink before we go. I had them make it special just for you." "No thanks Eve. I think I might be allergic to cranberry juice. And besides there's a dead fly in it." "Oh, Stewart, I thought you liked Cape Codders...and that's not a dead fly. It's the end of the stirrer at the bottom of the glass." "Well, that was sweet of you Eve. I've been *cutting down* lately, thank you." "Yes, Stewart. So I noticed."

Speaking of notice; as in taking notice and paying attention to the changes taking place around us. Hasn't everyone realized what a shitty mess the country's in? Is anyone taking the Republican nominations seriously? Harold treats this period in our history as curious subject matter; insisting that this whacked decade is a transition phase. The only news of note is the trinity of female saints that are either awaiting canonization or the prime candidate in a future election. Mother Theresa, Princess Diana and Secretary of State, Hillary Clinton are the nominees in that order. It was their dedication, personal sacrifice, and forgiveness that held them high above their secular counterparts. Miracles still surround them. Indian paupers, crippled and ill, rise, walk and are cured at the mention of Mother Theresa's name. Diana still conjures a belief in Cinderella, though no longer the possibility of Anglo-Egyptian diplomatic ties. Most of all, forgiveness has triumphed over adjuration for the once disgraced Hilary whose husband's cigar got him in trouble. Hillary's Bill has survived his former scandal, and Hilary may still have her day. Seinfeld is gone, yet he reminded us of the many uses of guilt and confirmed the intransigence of the American character traits of self-ridicule and high a school locker room mentality. Virtues that still have purpose today. He also serves to remind us that everything about which he - and we – have concerned ourselves is much to do about nothing in particular. Mothers Theresa, Diana, and Hillary save me from my cynicism! Done. Back to the lighter Seinfeld side of the Ashley dancers...

This is not a guide to dance, a religious treatise or a pitch for any particular political party. This is a magnum copes whose title might should read: "DESCENDANTS OF THE LOST ARK FOUND. THEIR MISSION ON EARTH: TO HELP AL GORE AND THE CORP OF ARMY ENGINEERS SAVE MANKIND FROM THE FLOOD THAT IS FORECASTED TO INUNDATE THREE-FIFTHS OF THE WORLD'S LAND MASSES IN THE YEAR 2012!" Yellow journal hyperbole? Don't be gullible, but *do* believe the Enquire and Globe press releases. It is interesting, isn't it though, that these mass distributed, widely read newspapers are based in Florida. It is almost as though they knew where to establish their headquarters, and await the arrival of the nation's saviors. Being close by to get a scoop, (skills once desperately in demand aboard the ark's lower animal deck), at the time in history when the eagerly awaited Revelations are about to come to pass. Hoss said that California was full up with crazies, and that Florida had room for some of the over flow. Which, he says, accounts for the increase in law practices, and prison construction as a major growth industry. Reverend Jack warns that it isn't safe to settle down on any of the seaboard coasts, and that we should all buy what will be ocean front property in Nevada and Alabama by the year 2020. Well I don't subscribe to any of this doomsday malarkey. However, I do like the climate in Las Vegas, and I'll miss the majesty of the Grand Canyon when it's filled with salt water, and the mafia renames it Grand Casino Bay and launches its gambling fleet that'll offer coast-to-coast entertainment. It'll be a short trip.

The most inauspicious day of the 90s was Thursday, July 30th, 1998. It marked the End Time and the coronation of the Beast. This was a sad day in history; when the Baby Boomers of America wore the black armband of mourning, and lamented the end of an era. On July 30th, "Buffalo Bob" Smith died. And so did the town of Doodyville, U.S.A. The mythical town in which I and millions of other American children grew up. Important as Camelot to the British and the Kennedys. Important as Shangri-la and Xanadu to the Shangrilalians and Xanadudes. Sad was the day when Wilder's, Main Street was bull-dozed to make way for a Super Walmart. Andy and Opie still whistle down the dirt road to Mayberry, but only in the re-runs. Howdy Doody (God rest his soul/hand of Bob) move over. Make way for Chucky - your replacement. The demented and homicidal alter-ego of the generation. The boyish apple-cheeked, freckled-faced innocence of Howdy, having once vanquished the sarcasm of Charlie Mc McCarthy, the evils of Froggy and His Magic Twanger, and the brazen coquetry of Madam, is gone for good. And I would be remiss if I were not to mention that the death of Sherry Lewis followed four days after "Buffalo" Bob's. But then again we're talking about the death of Lamb Chop - a lamb (Webster's Dictionary defines lamb as, 1 a: a young sheep; esp.: one that is less than one year old or without permanent teeth). I'm sorry but sheep has a connotation that is antithetical to the Doody generation.

Being one of the sheep is not a flattering association. Count sheep to go to sleep. Wake up Howdy fans. Be counted. "What time is it, boys and girls?" Why, it's Howdy Doody time...regrettably, no more. Face the fact, Howdy's dead and the Evil Puppet Master is loose upon the country once again.

Praise the Hindu gods, for the cultural icon that is the Ashley. This is no mere place in the physical plane of places and things. The Ashley is the lodestar upon which the New Generation will set its course for the future. Now it's Reverend Jack who's become skeptical. His support is with the qualification that we should still move to the "new west coast" as soon as possible. And Eve was emphatic about not traveling aboard an Ark with a bunch of terrible dancers. So unlike the Irish traveling steerage on the Titanic who could, at least, dance away the final, fateful hours before they met their end.

There is doomsday anxiety associated with the second decade of the 21st century. And you know how men will exploit the opportunities of war and see advantages associated with the panic surrounding an imminent doomsday. You know the pitch, 'Honey, this may be our last evening together. The meteor is predicted to impact earth tomorrow, and the flood waters are rising. There's no place to hide. All life on earth will be destroyed. Let's make this night special, so our love will last forever.' Translated: 'You've held me off for six months. I'm horny as hell. Don't make me wait till we are married. I'll never make the commitment. The frustration is killing me.' The wired generation has a knack for getting more to the point. They're direct, and ask for what they want. Encounters are brief, mating is swift. Dude meets Chick. Dude *or* Chick says, 'Hey ya wanna fuck?' The other, thinking about it, asks, 'Do you practice safe sex (meaning, 'Did you bring the condoms? I forgot.')?' By the mid-90's love bartering moved to the chat rooms of the World Wide Web. Boy could then ask girl for a virtual date. Similar risks attended: at the risk of having to commit to a binary relationship; and risk being infected with a computer virus. Fortunately a Disk Doctor and an Anti-Virus Shield can provide protection against a multitude of unwanted cyber infections. A crashed system is the equivalent of a messy divorce. My hunch is that only a fraction of the Ashley patrons are computer literate and chat room active. The majority is computer celibate, and prefers taking the risks associated with dating and marrying with reckless abandon in real time. To them an ego devastating rejection, an STD or a messy divorce followed by financial ruin is less confusing than manipulating their mouse in the ethers of frustration.

The cultural explosion that was the sexual revolution in the sixties is only faintly echoed in the contemporary sexual psyche. Once sex was friendly and maybe even on the side of women; meaning that sex was free of pregnancy and of disease. Eve accuses me of being an outmoded libertine with a selective memory. She had the audacity to remind me that I was deathly afraid of catching a cold from a date, and that the thought of catching the clap aroused the fear of being exiled to an island off the coast of Guyana by the Dade County Health Department. I had let it slip once that her stash of penicillin that I found when we were dating made me afraid to date her, even though she insisted that she was hoarding it for a trip to India where medical supplies were scarce. Well forget it. Because Eve's spin on the historical facts doesn't change the big picture in which my legitimate medical concerns no longer play a significant part. The point I'm trying to make here is that something has changed regarding the sexual politeness that the sexes had once expressed toward one another. It seems as if there has been a backlash that has made the boudoir a battle zone, and misogyny a national past time equaling the attention men give to Football season. Of course there's been a violent female response to this as you might expect. A combination of PMS and an emotionally unavailable husband (football season and pre-mature andropause) is an instant legal acquittal when the 'poor woman bereft of her sanity due to her husband's cruel neglect,' justifiably dulls the machete on the heartless bastard. So you see, war is endless. And war has finally been declared between the sexes.

   Fortunately, war between the sexes hasn't been declared at the Ashley. It is a neutral zone, like Switzerland. Why? Because the sexual experiment that failed for most of the Western World succeeds in Stuart, Florida. What is it that has succeeded? Androgyny, that's what. The merger of the genders that makes GI Harold and Jane indistinguishable; except when (questionably) naked.

David Morgan is gender reversible, and he's damn proud of it. Reverend Jack began lecturing me about my, 'amoral, open-minded, permissiveness. The kind of non-committal stand that leaves the door ajar for the Devil to enter.' Jack launched a fundamentalist assault on David's 'sexually liberal persuasions; tantamount'n to turpitude.' Jack attacked David's open predilections toward romantic involvement with both genders as heathen –possibly Greek - bi-sexuality. And he accused David of cross-dressing just because he wore hot pants and a halter top to the Halloween party. Jack, crossing his legs in the protective manner of a homo-phobic, squinted with malice and invited the Lord's wrath upon David's loins. He scared Eve and I one evening when he produced a pair of castration sheers like the kind they used on Peter Abelard in the movie, *Saving Heaven*. I prefer a less judgmental and less sanguinary approach to 'YMCA' men like David. Eve and I are accepting of David's colorful fashions and his unconventional dating. For example, when David walks in arm-in-arm with Charlie

McQueen, Eve's inclined to remark, "That Charlie's a hunk. He's really built...he's put a lot of work into developing those pectorals and gluteus muscles. He and David look bitchin." To which I reply, yeh, uh'huh." On another Friday night when David walked in with Julia Van Chenin hanging at his side, I'm inclined to casually remark, "what a piece of ....gluteus muscle she is. Julia's built like a brick...edifice. Do you think David knows they're implants?" In response, Eve spears me with the repartee, "Yeah, I'd bet you'd have found that out about one minute after being introduced. Go ahead go ask her if you want. I won't be here when you get back." "Eve, I'm just commenting on David's good taste. They look great (meaning David and Julia of course) together. I think his immune system must be accepting the kidney." And besides we both had to agree that David looked as good in his tartan kilt as any Highland Scotsman. His legs are as shapely and as hairless as Julia's. And I dare say, as nicely toned, hot waxed, and well proportioned.

I realize that I've run the ark thing into the ground. Eve's gotten bored with the concept, while Reverend Jack's interest has peaked since our discussions began. His interest in the ark theory, as it were, inspired Jack to register Republican after decades of having cast the Independent vote. Eve says I should be ashamed - and afraid - for having stoked Jack's militancy and for being responsible for sending Jimmy Swaggart another soldier to fight the Holy War. As you know Eve can be very direct and hurtful with the truth. Her predilection to criticism isn't clouded by sentimentality or the rules pertaining to fair fighting in relationships. Fortunately, not all of my personal therapy has been successful and I've been able to preserve a lot of my denial. I've even managed to fully exonerate myself of any blame in the matter concerning Jack's conversion to millennium madness, because Jack is his own person even if he does attend Tea Party rallies, and wears a uniform that makes him look like a senior citizen doing a bad Michael Jackson impersonation. Well, I've begun playing it safe by avoiding Jack who is now a campaign volunteer at the office for Martin County Young Republicans. It's rumored that he's also been leading church services out of the store front where they are headquartered. He still frequents the Ashley; an obligation that he views as missionary work. As for myself, I go there because it's a nice relaxing break at the end of a strenuous work week. And also because, I take comfort among its patrons, who like me, are dance disabled when under the spell of the Ashley. This understandably frustrates Eve who loves to dance. She is so desperate for a dance partner that she's willing to lie to me. She'll look me dead in the eyes and tell me that I'm a wonderful dancer, and, yes, the next time that we dance she'll let me lead. So, I accompany her to the dance floor where there's a decent dance band…that's wasted on a man with the *potential* to boogaloo with the best of them…and can't. Well wouldn't at the time. And absolutely not at the Ashley. So before you start feeling sorry for Eve for want of a dancing husband, and wonder why she hadn't left me for another man who can dance, you need to know that I have danced with Eve on many, or rather quite a few occasions. Now my dance debut at the Ashley is another story. And the reason Eve wouldn't even consider accepting an invitation to dance from an Ashley dancing man is because she values her life, limb and marital fidelity. Most modest and happily married women would probably avoid the perversions to which they would be subjected on a dance floor that resembles the romper room at a Plato's Retreat.

You should have been here in the summer during the "Dancing in the Streets" festival - which is held coincidentally when the blue land crabs migrate. And this isn't an intentionally obtuse reference, i.e., equating a crab migration to "Dancing in the Street." These two events, however, are related. The forces of nature act strangely and profoundly on both the crustaceans, and on the patrons of the Ashley. Both crustacean and patron are tugged by gravities that are far beyond their ability to understand much less control. If the advertising for "Dancing in the Streets" hadn't been advertised so long the event took, it would have been postponed until after the crab migration. I know and you know that migrations aren't precise events. The crabs don't keep time or regulate their mating cycles to clocks, calendars and thermometer readings the way we do. They just seem to know instinctively when it's time to fall in, march and mate. And they don't care exactly when it is, where they do it and who's watching...just like the typical Ashley dancer. While thousands of crabs were exiting their borrows and crossing streets in search of salt water (in which they indiscriminately pair up and mate), the visitors to down town Stuart were competing with the crabs on the same thoroughfares of travel. And those who made it to the Ashley converged upon the dance floor and intermingled like crabs in the throes of passion. When the crabs make it to water they spawn hundreds of eggs to ensure the survival of their species. So few actually survive. Many are crushed beneath the automobile tires of homicidal anti-conservationists. Environmental war criminals who, one day soon I expect, will face long prison sentences for the sick pleasure they've taken in blinding the beady-eyed crustaceans in their high beams and mowing the side-skedaddling, tire- puncturing, lower-life-forms down (Yes, I do think some of them deserve it). Other predators have their way with the rest. A similar fate often awaits the careless person who ventures blindly onto the dance floor of the Ashley. Blinded by the mirrored disco ball, and confused by the choreography of the Electric Slide, the dancing duo (not a requirement at the Ashley) might be handled, fondled, trampled and flattened...And discouraged from ever returning to Ashley to dance again. To prevent the crippling of the patrons - and to encourage an ambulatory, return business - Hoss and Annie conceived the idea of sponsoring, *"The Millennium Dance Contest."*

CHAPTER 9

do you want to dance?

"I am punishing her because she did not dance for you. People in our position should learn early how to please. Her stubbornness could have lost me my job and taken away the love that you have for her. Whatever you ask, it is for us to do."

[Senior Quintero's housekeeper, Luz, explaining to him why she punished her six year old daughter, Rosario]

From, <u>If You Don't Dance They Beat You</u>
By, Jose Quintero

...And that's how I feel today when I'm asked to dance. Like poor little Rosario. When I was five years old my mother and my aunt took me and my cousin Billy to a dance studio in Philadelphia and paid the studio director to teach us to dance. I think they were grooming us to appear on American Bandstand. But I don't recall seeing mirrored walls and a waist high rail around the dance floor of American Bandstand. The lady at the studio kept goading me into holding onto the rail with one hand while raising the opposite leg into the air in the most painful stretch-BVD position that I had ever experienced. I immediately felt like a ballerina, and after removing my wedgie, I snapped to military attention and refused to cooperate further. Even at the age of five the idea of donning a tutu aroused an acute gender identity panic. My mother's coaxing, having been met by my defiance only piqued her anger. Her anger I think caused her embarrassment because my mother hated to lose her temper in public, so she feigned composure and offered me a bribe. She told me she'd buy me a toy motorcycle (a boy toy) if I'd *just try and dance* (a girl thing). Well I negotiated poorly at five; refusing *to try,* and still wanting the toy as payment for damages. Instead of my mother taking me to the University of Pennsylvania and enrolling me in their law school, she dragged me the length of a city block. She moved with quick strides, hurrying us past the shops of the South Street vendors to the bus stop where PS bus #33 whisked us home. When we got in the house I remember my mother sulking in front of the TV and watching the kids dance to the music of American Bandstand. 'How proud of them their mothers must be,' she muttered out loud. A harsh note of disappointment in her voice.

    You can understand why, from this troubling incident in my childhood, I might cringe at the thought of *having* to dance. There are worse things a person might have to do than to dance under duress, but I can't think of any. If I had to come up with something I'd compare it with the abuses to which some people subject themselves in the name of religion. Like trundling along on your knees across a stone covered courtyard the length of a football field to pay homage to the Hindu temple gods. Or being asked to dance by Halal al-Din al-Rumi the Dervish. Everyone has this idea that dance has its origin in fun, free movement and the unfettered expression of the human spirit. History instructs us to choose our dance floors carefully. Dance has been performed in the interests of war (war dances), the formal mating rituals of birds and savages, and for communicating the code of the culture. Hence, the revival of the ancient hula, the Lakota Sun Dance, etc., etc.

    I read an obit announcing the recent death of Helen Hoakalei Kamauu who is credited with leading the revival of kahiko, the ancient hula. She insisted that her students precisely follow the kahiko steps and chants. No more hip wiggling, grass skirted beauties immortalized for me as the automobile dash novelty that shimmies to the motion of stops and starts. Helen had to come along and ruin things. Just like the airlines when they started hiring mature flight attendants of all body types. Same with Helen. Now a fat girl could put on a skirt the size of a multi-family hut, and gyrate hips the width of out riggers. As long as she could manage all of this without setting her ass on fire with blazing torches borrowed from the statue of Liberty. One pelvic thrust out of synch with a big bellied chant, and the whole dancer could go up in smoke and incinerate most of the spectators along with her.

Remember the western movie when the gunslinger bully would tell the scared and defenseless kid to dance to the bam!, bam!, bam! of bullets fired at his boots. Well I could go on and on...and I will. Because I intend to expose dance for what it really is...a feminist plot to make men sterile (like bicycle riding).

What a woman does to a man when she drags him onto the dance floor is...expose him. Exposes his feminine side, as it's euphemistically called, in front of everyone. Which means he is caught up in the shameful act of moving his hips, rolling his shoulders and taking dainty little steps to music. The music and lyrics to which are performed and written by pimple faced kids from Seattle whose sperm count is negligible because of all of the potent hydroponic ganja they've been smoking since elementary school. I am convinced that guys don't like any of this, as much as we will pretend to like it just to please our dance partner. And also because I remember my mother lying to me; telling me, 'If you learn to dance, the girls won't leave you alone. Girls are really attracted to boys who can dance.' They know how gullible we are. They know that we'll do stupid and dangerous things for a woman's praise. Even dance.

This reminds me of the 1988 movie, "Frantic", starring Harrison Ford and Betty Buckley. There is this unforgettable dance scene. It is by far the worst dance scene ever filmed in the history of American cinema. It is a dance that many men have experienced. It requires: a. one man trying to keep a low profile like Harrison Ford who, in this particular scene, is attempting to avoid the notice of medical colleagues in a bar in Paris; and, b. your average female, illegal contraband courier (who can be found working as a waitress at the Ashley while under probation supervision) who can't sit still to music. So here is Harrison Ford leading Betty by the hand out of this bar and very much in a hurry. And while he's making a bee line for the rear exit, he makes the mistake of crossing the dance floor. This is Betty's cue to have a dancing spasm that strikes Harrison with catatonia. And while Harrison is stunned and confused, Betty takes the liberty of dancing with him with neither his conscious awareness nor his willing participation. By God, when Harrison regained his senses the startled expression on his face was no acting job. He had become the incapacitated prey of a female anaconda in heat. One that writhed, climbed, slithered, hissed and squeezed him with powerfully muscled thighs that wouldn't quit. Had this been the adagio, Harrison would have been tied, beaten, garroted, shot and left for dead right there on the floor. The fact that he lived through the scene was no blessing. Harrison learned his lesson well because in later films he'd head for the dugout of dance and refuse to play. He defended himself admirably as Dr. Jack Ryan in Clear *and Present Danger*. It was in the next to final scene when he replied insubordinately to his boss, the President of the United States (who had insisted that Jack play the game and 'dance the Potomac two-step'). To which Dr. Jack Ryan replied, 'No thank you sir. I don't dance.'

That scene with Betty though aroused so much dance anxiety that Eve responded with sympathy and let me sit out the next Friday night at the Ashley without rebuke. It was the first time in a long time that Eve didn't lay on the parting guilt trip with, "well, we can leave now since you aren't going to dance with me". But of course sympathy has a short half-life, especially with a woman who is a frustrated adagio dancer. One whose vengeance had finally begun to peak after eighteen years of unrequited dance. Eve's revenge was made possible, as well as that of hundreds of other women, by the sponsors of the Millennium Dance contest, Hoss and Annie Dodge. Their brainstorm to host a dance contest put Stuart on the map. To top it off, Good Morning America filmed their show live from the Ashley following the owner's announcement. The Dodges were the forerunners of a take-off hit in evening TV entertainment. Their brainstorm launched future programs like, *Dancing with the Stars*, and *You think you can Dance*. But, I'm getting ahead of myself.

So, let's call this exploration of the Ashley phenomenon, a psychological thesis on dance, with relevant political and biblical postscripts supporting key findings. Along with it I have added an incautious criticism of a certain political party's, right wing leanings, comparable to the rise of Fascism in the early twentieth century. You may find this rationale specious from an historical viewpoint. Nevertheless, you will agree that Newt Gingrich does resemble Heinrich Himmler and Fatty Arbuckle. Several sacred institutions have been desecrated by my sacrilegious aping. It's my way of extorting agreement from less radical, political sympathizers and agnostics. And, it just so happens, that the political party I have offended is the enemy of the people known as the Ashley dancers. The blood-line descendants of the Eighth Ark who have forgotten their history, lapsed into political lassitude, and had gotten lost along the way.

Hoss and Annie did their homework in planning the Millennium Dance Contest. They had encouraging success with a rehearsal hosted by Charlie Mc Queen at his palatial river house. It was 'By Invitation Only.' Charlie personally invited Eve and I to attend. He shares my concern for the impending Apocalypse, and, like myself, he isn't taking any chances. He wants to have the right people around, not *if*, but *when* the time arrives. It didn't surprise me to see a large vessel moored at Charlie's dock that resembled that *darting little sloop with filigree decorations in sandalwood all along the stern*. It annoyed Eve that I was making *the* analogy again. And besides, it was Charlie who came up with the title for the event. I was honored to be included in the 'guest manifest.'

   The pent- up party energies of Charlie's guests was awesome. The ones who left early were simply overwhelmed by the sight of people having so much fun bopping in triple time to slow, dance music. Dr. Ricardo and his new (third) wife, Trudy, left soon after their arrival; exiting with a quick, compulsory polite hi and goodbye. One reason being, I suspected, was because Trudy's multiple body piercings were being drawn and bent to the magnetism of a crowd whose collective gauss strength was powerful enough to curl a meat cleaver. And rumor had it that Trudy was pierced in all of her major erogenous parts. Eve got ticked, telling me that that metal bending parlor trick was a hoax perpetrated on a naive public by that charlatan, Uri Geller. And that Trudy's discomfort was due to slow healing which wasn't helped by the pressing crowd and rising body heat, caused by an unseasonably hot summer and Dr. Ricardo's frisky attentions.

Hoss' and Annie's long experience with identifying talent and managing hospitality services had paid off. Their pick of the bands and their skill with event planning was par excel lance. They knew their clientele. They knew they weren't the Key West set, and the adept 'Duval Crawlers' who could master the swaggering march from bar to bar. Their patrons didn't possess the faculty to produce the necessary retarding effects of alcohol or the displaced mental state of a tourist as the excuse for dancing poorly or behaving foolishly.

The Ashley patron is the in-bred, indigenous people of downtown Stuart. Having returned to the cradle of their original home. Guided by inexplicable cosmic forces and plentiful Dance Contest advertising; the timing of which was no mere coincidence. Hoss and Annie sponsored several starter events that brought in the regulars and ensured, through various forms of blackmail, that the disenfranchised would attend the grand reunion. The marquis in the display case by the front doors listed the schedule of events for the month leading up to the dance contest. The advertising read as follows:

R.J. Rowling Book Burning- Bonfire Party	Sat. 11/3/2012
Drag Queen Party (Private: Invitation Only)	Sun. 11/11/2012
Slam Poets' Open Mike Night - $200 Grand Prize	Sat. 12/17/2012
Millennium Dance Contest - $500 Prize, Worst Couple	Sat. 12/26/2012

With program entries like these, you just knew something big was brewing. And guess who was behind the, 'Bonfire Party?' You were right if you guessed the Martin County Young Republicans. Actually, Jack solicited the group playing on Hoss' fear about too much government. He misrepresented the group's agenda by concocting a story about an overstock of Rowling's books that were going to the recycling plant. So why not use them for a bonfire, and save the trees from being chopped into firewood. Hoss ultimately relented to Reverend Jack's gentle persuasions. Truth be known, Hoss would have favored burning the pages of Facebook if it were published in paperback instead on scattered throughout the ethers. He is troubled by the fact that his name, buying habits, medical and credit histories are available to anyone inclined to Google his name. But then so is yours and mine. Jack was on a mission and he was shrewd enough to disguise his warped intentions by offering to be their generous contributor.

Like most of the Reverend's schemes which are essentially harmless, this one was not. He had become a closet neo-Nazi. The antithesis of his former peace and love mantra. Perhaps Jack actually lacked the faith he so extolled, and didn't have a whole lot of faith in the American knack for being able to solve the big problems any longer.

So, he felt justified in picking on young warlocks whose only sin was cheating with wizardry to best the evil sorcerer's in the British parliament. He was as faithless in the year 2000 when the Y2K scare paralyzed the nation with fear that their computer programs would revolt. Even though the problem was fixed, no one in their right mind, including the Jack, would book a flight on New Year's Eve. He withdrew everything from his bank accounts and liquefied his investments. He regressed and hid his assets amid the socks and underwear in his dresser drawer which he referred to as his *stash*. He was ready to toss new logs on the bonfires over that scare. It would have been hard drives. Jack is still worried, kike Hoss, that he is a traceable number. And when his social security number is inputted by the government monitors, his secrets are reveled. His insatiable appetite for Christian choir music, chatting on Tiny Tots Match.com, and orders from the High Times catalogue - a secret no more. He relished the thought of burning all those hard drives, the noxious fumes' mile-high plume of toxic soot notwithstanding. Jack would have to be satisfied, this century, with destroying the evil reading that would erode the morality of our Tot generation, and bring the nation down. Jack would no doubt dance (or try to) around that bonfire! You will have to imagine for now: The Reverend Jack as black as a tar baby from standing downwind of the smoke plume, and chanting slogans like a book burner at a Nazi rally. He would be spared the toxins of the poly-carbon-fluorocarbons, and have to be satisfied the clouds of burning books tainted with acid treated paper and lead-laced printers' ink. Many will join him I'm certain. Thrilled to join him in the song and dance (badly, out of tune and step) to the music of an old Seattle band.

The bonfire event is a bad idea. But it is by no means the only novel extravaganza ever put on by the Downtown merchants. The most bizarre one by far, but not the only popular venue. Every other event takes up the entire two-block area comprising downtown Stuart. The Ashley is always at the center of things. *Dancing in the Streets* and *The River Daze* festival are fun activities. But a bonfire on the riverbank attended by a mad minister and a Tea Party delegation? In a word (x 3): weird, weird, and weird. And portentous.

As a hip and tolerant person, you might say that a drag queen party is no big thing, right? Every city has its campy gay entertainment. And the drag queen mecca is in Key West, the tail end of the Florida peninsula; one-hundred and fifty miles south of here as the pelican flies. So why not Stuart? A problem developed because Ashley patrons of every sexual stripe wanted to participate. They asked the perfectly Constitutional question, 'why can't we come too?' And come they did. A hundred-and-fifty people arrived; out-numbering the bona fide gay crowd twenty-to-one. And more of the straight people arrived in drag than did the gay partiers. And do you know who took the prize? And then took one another home afterwards? David Morgan and "The Reverend" Jack, that's who. I shit you not. The clincher was David dressing to the tees and being a dead ringer for Justin Bieber. The on-line data base may have had Jack pegged with regard to his preferences. Anyway, the gay community was out-raged. They told Hoss they were taking their business to Key West in the future. I told Eve that I thought Jack was behind the Ashley Drag Queen Party takeover. At first she expressed doubt, but after she thought about it for a minute she met my steady gaze with affirmation. 'You don't mean that Jack has hatched another right wing conspiracy to cleanse the race by posturing as a drag queen?" "Yes I do Eve. That Grand Old Party troublemaker may have pulled one over on them. Even if it were a clever charade, Jack was convincing. He sure looked the part in that taffeta teddy." "Yes,

Stewart, but the glitter makeup sticking to all that body hair was a little tacky, don't you think?" "Yeah, he should have had the good fashion sense to have shaved, plucked his eyebrows and bikini waxed before setting his jellies through the door."

After the drag queen party, the Slam Poets' Open Mike competition was a most welcomed relief. Even if it is populist art. Meaning it doesn't have to be good, just successfully marketed. And, as populist poetry, it isn't bound by any of those unreasonably strict poetry guidelines. Like the one's imposed on aspiring poets by those foppish literary journals and magazines that cater to intellectuals. With Slam, anything goes; nothing is sacred. Attack racism, the Disney Corporation, chauvinism or feminism. And yet the toughest part is keeping score at a Slam's wild competition. This is very tough considering that scoring is done by judges who are usually selected randomly from the audience. The ESPN junkie makes the best judge because of his aptitude for keeping up with scores. After all, Slam got its name in the '80s from a guy by the name of Mark Smith...who was, it is fabled, thinking of an Ernie Banks home run. And so named it after Ernie's grand slam. Thank goodness Mark wasn't in the men's room or the team locker room when the name-that-poetry inspiration struck him.

And they be poets, nonetheless...

"Put some poets, slam poets under that heat, and anything goes. They might faint or cry or tear off their shirts. They might whisper in a crowded bar or shout "YEE-HAH" in a crowded theater. They might nitpick like a pack of lawyers or hug like they'll hang on forever."

"Slam Poets speak to a new generation of beat"
Article by AP Writer, Hillel Italie

Of all the open mike nights that feature local talent, the Ashley Slam entries were a big hit, and seemed to speak the language of the regulars. Hell, anybody can rhyme words, and master the Ebonics vocabulary just by attending Florida public schools. But the Ashley devotee personifies Slam. Slam may have been officially born in a Chicago bar in the '80s and traveled the commercial mainstreams through the states of America and the provinces of Canada, but it's a fact that it's been a living language since the original Ashleys, Mobleys and Lowes drew breath, babbled and crawled. It is possible that the Ashley Gang first invented Slam when Hanford Mobley dressed in drag, entered the bank with his two accomplices, pointed like a preacher and shouted at the tellers and the crowd, 'Dis be a robbery. Gib me all da dough.' And plead'n wid his accomplices whilst exiting da joint, 'And if da take be real puny, don't yous guys be cappin me like dat rat did...Kid Lowe.'

This just goes to show you that nothing new arrives on the modern scene that hasn't already been introduced by our great-grand-daddies. Perhaps it is because this fact eventually surpasses all novelty, that apathy has become epidemic, and boredom has become a popular past time. A condition which portends the beginning of the end. And I do believe that it was desperation caused by boredom and the sameness of everyday life that set in motion the events that I'm about to describe. They happened just as I'm about to describe. And it all came to a climax at the Millennium Dance contest. An event that offered new found hope, saved the day...and redeemed the sorry-ass, lifeless marble that this world had become.

"Born during the Renaissance, cafe society was the source of many of the changes that formed our modern world. The coffeehouse was where political revolutions in England, France and Russia were nurtured and planned; where such revolutions in art and literature as Dadaism, futurism, surrealism, cubism, and existentialism were formulated and developed; and where such theoretical disciplines as psychoanalysis and modern physics were brought to life."

From, <u>Espresso</u>

By, Petzke and Slavin

The Ashley as the cradle of creativity will have a peaceful revolution set to the call of a Gillespie trumpet riff, not the bugle. Not to a goose-step in storm boots, but with *something* passing for dance. You will spin your partner dozy doe, twirl in unison with your disco date, and hokey- poky around the rink on your roller skates. Getting dizzy? The Ashley has always been the place where new and unusual things happen. And where it continues to happen on a regular basis. Where the off-beat dance...well, dance off beat. Hoss and Annie are about to exploit these dance antics and host a contest that dared to reward the *worst dancers*, which they knew was the best that the Ashley dancers could do. First there were the *Biggest Losers,* and now the Winning Worst Dancers. Now there's an idea for new TV series.

"Tricks, tips, and philosophies that will help both the student and the professional dancer vault the 40-year barrier and live a long life in dance. A dance legend writes about diet, sex, dangers, healers, making a living, and, most important, the heart-mind of the dancer who survives."

> From, <u>How To Dance Forever Surviving Against The Odds</u>
> By, Daniel Nagrin

The author of the book, whose excerpts are quoted here, is one of the country's most distinguished and acclaimed *solo* dancer and choreographer. Note the adjective, *solo*. Come on, Dan. You're more likely to survive on the battlefield of the dance floor if you dance alone. Now try dancing with a partner at the Ashley. That is if you're the reckless type whose inclined to take risks; unafraid of being lamed or laughed at. Then write the sequel:

.

"Trips, flips and catastrophes are certain
to be*fall* the beginner or the professional
dancer who is foolish enough to tango at the
Ashley. If you do, then do so, at your peril.
A dance legend warns - take heed:
Be brave; act nonchalant when being groped
by strangers; do not mistake your
dance partner for one of the living; and, most
importantly, see your doctor before attempting
to follow any of the dances being performed
by others. The loss of a limb, or your virginity
will be the least of your concerns."

From, <u>Dancing At The Ashley</u>
<u>Flirting With Sudden Death</u>
By, Daniel Chagrin

Dancing alone isn't an option. In fact it's strictly against the rules. You will be required to select a partner, and take her or him, or either, or to the dance floor, where you will be essentially a tall stick of dynamite dancing with Helen Kamauu's protégée. And guess what else, Dan? Her big grass skirt's on fire. And... she has the hold-on staying power of Betty Buckley. Survive that, and live the rest of your shortened life with a hurt that won't quit.

    I wish I had known all of this before I'd written about it. Because if I had, a warning to the unsuspecting might have helped spare a few people. More might have survived the fate which awaited them. Well, we learn from experience. But unfortunately, no such prior experience existed which might have helped us prepare for what lie ahead. The only ones who probably did know what lie in store for us were the descendants of the Eighth Ark...And they were very stingy with their knowledge. And they flat out refused to share their knowledge with the uninitiated. And for their meanness, on this - their return trip - they would get their just dessert. And so they did, for the price they paid, far exceeded the admission fee to the dance contest of the millennium. It was very, very great indeed.

CHAPTER 10

the millennium dance contest!

I cringe as the week-end approaches because Eve's growing more and more excited about the dance contest at the Ashley this Saturday night. It's only Tuesday and she's going on and on about how she and I are going to win. She's already spent the $500 prize money on various and sundry home improvements. I should be flattered that she has that much confidence in me as her dance partner. No sooner do I entertain the thought when I realize that Eve's confidence is being bolstered by my absolute lack of confidence. Moreover, it is upon my ineptness on the dance floor that she has declared a premature victory and spent the prize money.

   It was my own fault for agreeing to enter the contest. I should have been a better listener and paid attention when she asked me. Although I don't remember saying that I would. That's because I was on the phone handling an emergency call put through to me by my answering service. It was, Evelyn, my suicidal patient with whom I had just talked out of overdosing on her husband's Viagra prescription. I had just helped Evelyn to understand that her wanting Harvey to find her dead, standing upright with a rictus grin on her face was an act of repressed anger. She agreed to punish Harvey by flushing his prescription down the toilet, and further tormenting him by running around the house naked and living to be a hundred. Evelyn had just thanked me for being there for her when she needed someone to talk to. It was probably during this intervention with Evelyn when Eve asked me if I would enter the contest with her. I had just answered Evelyn, "Why, it's no bother, you know I'm here for you when you need me." Eve swears I was looking right at her when I said it. There was no retracting my so-called acceptance. Eve had access to all our prescription medications. Like the ones that help you keep the lid on a lot of repressed feelings.

"To choose to be a [professional] dancer
is a lovely act of defiance."

Daniel Nagrin

To choose to dance at the Ashley is an act of defiance
that isn't pretty. Picture the two-year old throwing a tantrum,
as the humiliated parent drags him out of the church service.

Mr. Chagrin (again).

Typically unfamiliar with satire, absent of pride, and heedless of warning, the bumblers of dance bought every available ticket. It was a sellout event. Eve bought our tickets from Hoss and Annie while shopping at Publix where they'd set up a ticket sales table by the store's entrance. She invoked the good neighbor policy the week before by having Hoss promise to reserve her two of the very sought after, first come, first served contestants' tickets. Eve had curtly refused my considerate; "when I can get to it later this week." offer to buy the tickets." Damn!

The 'heedless of warning' refers to the dire predictions surrounding December 26, 2012 – the official Doomsday. Phenomena of all apocalyptic manner from a polarity shift involving the magnetic poles, to increased sunspot activity were prophesied to conclude the world's end. Science had conspired with religion – and finally replaced it – to make global warming, and interstellar anomalies the sword of a vengeful Jehovah. A class-off-the-chart hurricane followed by coastal flooding was the peril chosen for Florida's god-wrought heathen cleansing. A hurricane was the likely destroyer - one arriving after the end of the hurricane season. The weather experts regarded the storm as being so a-typical that they chose to ignore it. This hurricane was born, like any other, off the coast of Africa. And…so the inevitable came to pass.

'hurricane ashley'

It sat brewing east of the Lesser Antilles, and was moving on a slow and erratic Westerly course. Landfall could be expected in about two weeks, but the experts were wagering that the storm would stall out and dissipate when it reached the cooler waters to the West. Where it would make landfall, if at all, remained anyone's guess. The last few hurricane seasons had been uneventful ones. There were three tropical storms. Only one was up-graded to a hurricane. That was Hurricane Albert. He had made a wet and windy nuisance of himself from Baton Rouge, Louisiana all the way to Barnegat Light, New Jersey before losing steam and huffing and puffing out to sea where it became a whisper of wind felt only by the distant ships and sea birds. Now, the year's first hurricane might make its debut on the southeastern seaboard. The Hurricane Center begrudgingly named it "Hurricane Bruce;" ignoring convention and starting the naming process with 'B' instead of "A." Because they had secretly used "A" already; having circulated an in-house memo at the National Hurricane Center, saying, 'this hurricane 'AIN'T' going to happen.' Yet, here it was coming our way, more or less. Following the example of official apathy, no one was paying particular attention to this late season up-start. Besides, Hurricane Bruce hadn't maintained a very stable storm pattern. Its eye had not been well defined, and it was loosely organized. It appeared to be making its way across the Atlantic like a cha-cha dancer. As hurricanes go it was a wimp with winds clocked at seventy-nine miles an hour. It wasn't a very macho hurricane. In fact, it had become the laughing stock of the National Hurricane Center. That was a mistake.

Hurricane Bruce as it turned out was a whoop ass hurricane disguised in billowing petticoats of circular clouds under which lurked the iron balls and kick ass clod hoppers of Conan the Barbarian. And Hurricane Bruce, a.k.a., Hurricane cojones Conan was here to bring a reckoning to those who would judge a hurricane by its name. In the last few days, Bruce's coordinates put him one hundred miles due East of the Martin County coast. He would become, in a matter of hours, a category 5 hurricane, and packing winds of one hundred and forty miles per hour. The weather service's warning came too late. No one was prepared. Hurricane Bruce would be a party crasher.

Like most everyone else, Eve and I paid little attention to, 'that storm out there.' I had been secretly practicing dancing all week.. You know, doing the moves in front of the full-length mirror when nobody's home. Doing plies the length of the living room in a black phantom cape to the soaring operatic music of Andrew Lloyd Weber. Loosening everything up, stretching, and cantilevering over low garden bed fencing on my way out to the carport. I even did those difficult pelvic rotations, booty shakes and deep-knee bends to hot Latin music; the kind of music that causes involuntary muscle spasms when you're sound asleep and the music's playing in your head. I even went so far as to think and act in terms of a dance researcher. Like Dan Nagrin proposed in his book. I opened to page 172, and there at the top of the page was question 8 from the chapter entitled, 'Questions Asking to Be Researched.' Dan was fixated on buns (the infomercial euphemism for asses). Dan shows his own ass, and says, I quote, 'There is a schism running through the entire dance field and it revolves around the buttocks. No, not what you are thinking. Here is a school whose battle cry is: *Firm those buns; Tighten your rump.* Others regard this as a false and unnecessary tension that produces back spasms, pressure on the sciatic nerve in the area of the piriformis and a multitude of woes...One very expensive therapist, who is the only one recommended by some hotshot New York orthopedic surgeons, is fierce about strong repetitive contractions of the anal sphincter while you're standing on the curb waiting for the green light. Can this matter of firming or relaxing be researched?...I had been taught, until as an aftermath of my knee operation I developed what was apparently a severe sciatic irritation...At this turning, grabbing those gluteal muscles began to feel wrong,...I gave up on that buttock tightening maneuver completely, *but I don't know how right that was or is* (Dan's italics).' Whoa, Dan. When you said, 'No, not what you are thinking,' you were reading my mind. However, schism, crack, buns, rump or ass, it was basically wise to put your research on hold. You'd be writing from prison by now, and, well, your research - I'm certain of this - would have continued behind (no pun intended) bars.

Hey look, Mr. Nagrin (this is a litigious world in which we live), I was just kidding. I think what you propose is an invaluable research question. Especially if I could be your research director and we started with the Dallas Cheerleaders. I really respect their callisthenic, athletic work outs. I think they would be excellent test cases. I'll persuade Eve to grant a marriage sabbatical for the year to take your research on the road. No, seriously. I have done what that very expensive New York therapist suggested. You know, 'the strong repetitive anal sphincter contractions.' I had to vary the routine though because we don't have to walk as much here in Florida because of our reliance on cars. So I did it in the car while stopped at red lights. The data is incomplete, though judging from the results; Eve has noticed fewer dimples through the seat of my tight fitting Levis and a pronounced truck to my gait. I'm also stingier and won't share my things as much as I used to - due to my improved anal retentiveness. I hate talking about these things, but I had to rely on a Metamucil cocktail or two after training. I am loath to admit it...I think it has helped my dancing. Eve said my walk reminds her of a matador approaching a bull. She knew something was up.

She may even have suspected that I had been practicing for the contest during off time. Ready or not, Friday night would arrive and I'd be ready (if I didn't come down with the flu, or pull a hamstring). Eve's excitement was far more contagious.

"They Shoot Horses Don't They"

Title of a 1969 Film

Starring Jane Fonda

That's the movie I had in mind while I was driving to the Ashley. It's was an association that I couldn't shake once we were on our way to participating in the contest. I can't say that I remember the details of the film. My memories connected with 1969 drift back in lazy motes of particle dust, paisleys and orange sunshine. I do remember this...it was not Jane and her date's high school prom, and it didn't have a happy ending. At least it didn't go well for her date (in the acting sense). So what's new? Jane Fonda was nominated as best actor. Her dance partner wasn't even nominated as best supporting actor. Jane, playing the role of Gloria Beatty, goaded her dance partner, Robert Syverton (played by Michael Sarrazin), into shooting her for having collapsed on the dance floor, and for being responsible for having them eliminated from a dance marathon upon which it seemed their lives depended.

The times are fickle. In the Depression era, when this event was to have taken place, a man might conceivably be provoked to shoot someone for failing to dance the distance. In the 21st century, dancing till you pass out or falling and getting knocked out is nothing to be ashamed about, much less getting shot over. What hasn't changed in seventy years is dance partner persecution. Note the fact that Jane led the whole time, and dragged poor exhausted Michael Sarrazin around like a rag doll with elastic foot straps attached to his feet. She *made* him dance against his better judgment in the first place. She commands Michael to shoot her. He obliges. And who really suffered? Worse, who ended up doing hard time for being obedient and doing just *another* bad thing that he was told to do. Hard time must have been easy compared to suffering through hours of grueling competition. I know these weren't good thoughts I was having. It was no way to approach, as Eve had put it, the fun and excitement that lay in store. Now, optimism I can fake. Dance is more difficult. And here I was, about to enter the Ashley to participate in a dance contest with Eve, my very own Gloria Beatty. Eve, or Gloria, to me they were the same. Eve, a.k.a., Gloria, was leading me to the Aragon Ballroom of my worst fears. It was a good thing for Eve that she had left the gun at home. I should have been armed. I'd have felt a lot safer walking into the Ashley - into *that* crowd, and on *that* particular night. One could have easily slipped past the metal detector at the door concealing a Glock, but the pat down by the bouncers would have gotten you caught and in trouble. I think they were expecting Rob Syverton to show. At ninety-one, Rob could still be out there competing, and still dishing out compassion like the Dr. Kevorkian of dance. Senior citizens aren't inhibited by age or walkers from seeking their equal opportunity for accidents on the dance floor.

Speaking of which, one of the first couples I noticed butting in line to be the first to confirm their reservation and be to issued their contest numbers, were old (literally) Ben Chapman and Grace Waverly. For the record, Ben is seventy-six, and Grace is thirty-something. Good for,...them. If I were to have wagered on the outcome of the contest, I'd have placed my money on them coming in last. Meaning, they were damn good. Perhaps Ben was inspired by his younger dance partner. He appreciated having someone who could see, hear and move a bit quicker and could take the lead. Ben also admires Grace's superior reflexes in dance and, I suspect, in many other areas of his life as well. He once told me that Grace was patient at the times when it really counted. He'd smile like a happy fool, and say things like, 'Grace's squeals of appreciation are music to my ears. Every movement is dance with Grace. She was aptly named.' Now understand this, Ben is deaf and Grace towers over Ben at six-foot-one. My guess is she weighs one-ninety. 'Ben sees Grace's inner beauty,' Eve tells me.

She said this after I described Grace and Ben in terms of their statistical differences. My hunch is that Ben is also visually impaired (blind). Their differences notwithstanding, Ben and Grace can dance and they did on the night of the Millennium Dance Contest. I still can't figure out why they entered. They just must like to dance. They must be crazy.

Enter Tiresias.

Tiresias: "...Call out Cadmus from the halls--"

Enter Cadmus.

Cadmus: "...Where must we go to dance, in which direction turn our feet and set our gray heads tossing?...I should not tire, all night or all day long, of striking the earth with the thyrsus. We have joyfully forgotten that we are old!"

Tiresias: "... I too feel like a stripling and shall undertake the dances."

Cadmus: And shall we be the only men in the land to dance for the bacchic god?"

Tiresias: "Yes, for only we are sane - the rest are mad... Will it be said that I have no shame for old age since I intend to crown my head with ivy and to dance? But the god has made no distinction, whether it is the young who must dance or the older man, but he wishes to have honors equally from all, counting no one apart in his desire to be magnified."

Euripides, *The Bacchae*

Ben is a dancing man. He had given up the pursuit of youthfulness ages ago. That is, until Grace came along and livened things up for him. Dance is CPR for Ben. It was Grace's gift of life support that had kept him dancing. Ben and Grace are like dog fish on the dance floor. They're territorial, smooth, yet elegant. They'll die if they sit still. They were out on the dance floor before the band began to play. They were warming up like athletes before the start of an event. I felt intimidated already. I wanted to pull Grace from his wiry embrace. I knew it would be like pulling the plug on an ICU patient's life-support system. I wasn't proud of the thoughts I was having, and I didn't share them out loud (this time) with Eve. I don't have any scruples about sharing them with you.

The band that performed the music for the Millennium Dance Contest was, BSR, our favorite. The letters of their band stand for, 'Best Sounds Revival.' This is a great band that can play the music of the 60s to contemporary with the authenticity of the original bands and song artists. The lead singer, Les Man, is the mockingbird of music. He's a virtuoso entertainer in the tradition of Jethro Tull, but doesn't resemble Fagan wearing his greatcoat in *Oliver Twist*. Les looks like Les, more or less. The variability depends on whether he's feeling modest or cold and decides to put on a tee shirt to cover up his tattooed, goose pimpled, lanky torso. Suffice it to say his range is awesome. And the other members of the band are no less grand.

    They were the best pick as the contest's band. Their repertoire would put every dancer to the test, and inspire every dance move. They presented a musical anthology you'd ordinarily have to order through one of the late night TV commercials. The one's that jack up the volume while you're making love on the sofa and coitus-interrupt the romance with, 'Not Available in Stores. Order Now With Your Visa or MasterCard.

Only $19.99 for four CDs, plus 7.99 S&H. This is a Limited Time Offer. Call Now to Reserve Your *Anthology of the Greatest Bands*. CALL NOW! 1-800- 666-6659, Yes, That's Right, 1-800-NONOOKY.' Eve would be off the sofa like a flash looking for the Visa and groping in the dark for the telephone. Better hearing it live at the Ashley where the interruptions aren't as exhausting and annoying. Though BSR, with the help of Hurricane Bruce, would be louder, more disruptive...and bring down the house.

The Ashley was abuzz with activity. It was a virtual nest of hornets. Filled with the queens and drones of dance whose wiggle and wing beat wasn't such a far out description of the dancing that would be taking place. There was electricity in the air; the kind of ozone sharpness that stings the wasabi regions of your sinuses. There was also no mistaking the signs of an approaching storm.

Eve and I paid little attention to that 'storm out there,' because Angie and Zack were visiting my mother on Cape Cod for a few days before the Christmas holiday. So our parenting instincts weren't in a state of high alert. If Angie and Zack were home, we'd have erred on the side of caution and stayed home. It was times like these that I really missed the kids. While the Ashley crowd poured in, and the contest soon to be under way, Hurricane Bruce was, more or less, cha cha'ing our way, feinting this way and pivoting that, keeping the hurricane trackers amused and confused. The atmospheric charge was infectious. The contestants were psyched. So many awfully bad dancers would make this contest a close call for the judges. It made the contestants delirious with confidence. They were sloppy drunk with confidence. They had tasted the bitter gall of failure to dance well their entire lives, and now it could count for sweet success. In failure there would be victory, at last! I was scared. I knew that if I could just let Eve lead (like always) and not fight it, we could lose. If I resisted, and allowed myself to be distracted by the other dancers, I could be responsible for a victory on the dance floor that would end in divorce. I was glad to see the others in my class arrive. I could stop flattering myself. The capital sins of pride and vanity were unfamiliar and unwelcome in this holy of holies.

Charlie Mc Queen and his motley crew swaggered in with Charlie looking like the old Zap Comix character, Captain Piscum. Charlie and crew had commissioned his sloop for the cruise to the Ashley. Charlie tied up at the city docks which is only a short walk to the Ashley. David Morgan hurried into the Ashley ahead of the others. He was a wild looking sight: shivering from the cold; wet to the skin; and windblown. Charlie had appointed him helmsman. He had apparently navigated under full sail; bracing the helm and leaning into a mean and chilly headwind the eleven nautical miles from Charlie's river house to the Ashley. He looked a sight. His red perm had exploded from his head. His wet kilt clung to his thighs, and the rest billowed from his behind like the fancy fantail of a fighting cock. He was the 'mad man from across the water.' The anti-freeze effects of Bushmills and the brackish river spray had kept him from becoming fast frozen. Although a terrible sight to lay eyes on, he was limber and ready to trot, hop and seriously sachet. Other strange and familiar merrymakers joined the party. The contest was about to begin.

Annie walked on stage, grappled with the microphone, and through hiss, and squelch welcomed the dancers to the First, and probably their last, Millennium Dance Contest. The volume dipped as she wished the contestants the best of luck. She reminded the entrants to fill out the waivers holding the Ashley harmless for what damages they might inflict on themselves or others. The waiver was a masterpiece of civil-suit lawyering. The layers of legal protection that it guaranteed the Ashley were deeper than the hidden pleasures beneath the petticoats of a Southern Belle. It was unquestionably the handiwork of the prestigious law firm of Dershowitz, Rogers, Bailey, Golden and Starr. Annie was very forward thinking, and she knew of the grave, attendant risks. She had seen these people dance before, which she once compared to the frozen horror of witnessing a terrible train wreck. Her mellifluous Trinidadian accent blended with the soughing of the strengthening winds being ushered to shore by Hurricane Bruce. The excitement was building, as was the tempest.

    Hoss introduced the band. It was Hoss' job to handle the entertainment and manage the support staff at the Ashley. His musical abilities made him a good talent scout. He had a knack for backing aspiring garage bands, and not a few of them began their stellar careers in the music studio behind his house. Hoss was no Brian Epstein. He would never discover the likes of the Beatles or the Rolling Stones. He'd come pretty damn close there for a while. He blew it this time by letting go of the reigns and contracting 'SMOG Entertainment' to manage the Millennium Dance contest. What is in a name, Shakespeareans? Quite a lot, indeed. Ralph Killian founded 'SMOG - which stands for Strange Men of Gomorrah – Entertainment, along with four other businesses. He created them through opportunism. In other words, if a tornado lifted the roof off of a house in Stuart one morning, The SMOG Emergency Construction and Repair Company was in business the same afternoon. If there was a performance at the Lyric Theater next Friday night, the SMOG Theater Ushers and Crowd Control Company was formed by Wednesday. Ralph would be offering their services to the theater manager first thing Thursday morning. You get the picture. Ralph had a company that offered more services than a Mexican bordello. Likewise, the recipient of SMOG's services often felt that he'd just been fucked. Ralph must have kept his tee-shirt iron-on decal presser hot for this one. His white-on-black *SMOG - MILLENNIUM DANCE CONTEST- OFFICIAL* tee-shirts were still warm off the press when Ralph and his eight minions arrived to officiate as master of ceremony, crowd control, judges and bouncers. Ralph and his SMOG militia looked like gargoyles placed too near an industrial smokestack. They epitomized menace. They were people who knew how to take control of a crowd. The Ashley patrons reacted with nervous whispers, and furtive glances as the SMOG staff took their posts throughout the bar. Their presence communicated foreboding...and evil personified. I told Eve, they made me feel like I was in grade school again, and the nuns had returned to enforce the discipline. And it looked like they had been working out at the weight pile and had substituted steroids for the Eucharist. Eve addressed me in that treacle sweet tone of hers - the way you talk to your great-grandmother whose lost her marbles - , "Stewart, it's just Ralph and the Serbian immigrants trying to make an honest living. You act weird when you're nervous. Lighten up. It's only a dance contest." Only a dance contest, ha! Eve has a way of minimizing a maximally, imminent catastrophe. Like the semi catching up to our rear bumper at eighty-five miles an hour on I-95. "Eve, watch out that semi's barreling down on us, and it's not slowing the least bit!" "Stewart, I have as much right to be on the road as he has." "Eve we're defenseless sitting here in the breakdown lane. Move it!...please? Your make-up looks fine." That's the panic I felt the night of December 26th. A glance toward the angels on the pedestals confirmed my premonition. Their heads were tilted skyward. A worried look was chiseled into their features that I hadn't noticed before. They were slightly crouched, wings tucked, ready to take flight. Ready to dodge the wrecking ball...again.

Ralph hopped up on stage just as Hoss finished his introduction in what looked like a hostile takeover. Reverend Jack was inching his way toward Eve and I and I heard him echo my sentiment, "Ralph, the little bastard, just like him to pull a coup d'état at the biggest amateur dance contest in history. He's the dance partner of the Beast." Eve cast a 'rescue me' glance my way; my cue to steer her away from Jack. Finally she tugged my sleeve, and said insistently, "STEWART!" It was useless. We weren't going anywhere.

Jack had an oily slickness which enabled him to move like a man-eel through a crowd jammed so tight that everyone had to inhale and exhale in unison in order to breath. Jack's moved along, with the speed of greased Teflon, and disappeared in the crowd. "He's acting creepy tonight," I commented. "Something's possessed the man, and it isn't a benevolent spirit." "Oh, Stewart, give it a rest. Everyone in this place is wired tonight. Jack's just being his lovable, annoying self." I was shocked. To be honest, it was rare to hear Eve use the word 'lovable' and 'annoying,' in the same sentence when describing Jack. The same way she often describes me. Jack must have meant something special to her, and she was too shy to admit it.

Ralph's a short man. Close to the average of the midget family on the *Little People* TV program. Svorgney had to toss him on stage. He didn't mean to knock Hoss off stage. It was an accident. Ralph's vaudeville entrance earned him applause. Hoss had somehow regained his cool. He had good balance, and escaped serious injury when he tumbled off stage by using his momentum to execute an expert aikido roll. After the laughter and the applause died down, Ralph cleared his throat, neared the microphone, stood on his toes and lowered it. He repeated, 'one, two, three, testing' a half a dozen takes, and then read the contest rules from a scroll of continuous feed computer paper six-feet long...

"Dancers (who was Ralph fooling?) I'd like to welcome you to the Second Millennium Dance Contest. I'm sorry. I meant the First, since most of you weren't able to attend the very First one. You'll have to ask Ben about it, Ha, Ha. Seriously, ladies and gentlemen and ladmen and gentlelads (Ralph, the Consummate social-gynecologist)...SMOG is proud to sponsor this unique event. We are also honored to be your hosts tonight...and as spokesman for SMOG Entertainment, I'd like to extend a special thanks to Hoss and Annie for being so gracious in allowing us to bring this event to their magnificent establishment [Ralph points to Hoss and Annie in the palm up gesture that invites applause from the spectators]...

Now, I'd like to take this opportunity to introduce the members of the SMOG team who will be judging the dance competition this evening. Seated at the table in front of me are, from my right, Certina Cescunerovnia, Vladistoc Qustavio, Hugsu Chang, Josef Madosse, Kristina Zsastakova and Patricia Murphy-Nabokoff. Before being depor...driven from their homeland, these esteemed individuals were involved in the advancement of the arts. They were the founders of the Croatian Dance Re-education Sanatorium. We are fortunate to have them here in America where they will be able to continue their work through a generous grant funded by the National Endowment For the Arts. Let's welcome our special guests with a round of

applause [the applause is delayed by a hesitation that signifies caution
and vigilance. The kind of paranoid vigilance that makes it difficult
for the bar's regulars to clap and remain alert to danger at the same time.

The sound of their clapping is muted by the shrill whistling of the wind
as the velocity of the approaching hurricane increases].

Dance maniacs (Ralph was getting closer to describing the crowd more
accurately), I know you're eager to get on with the contest. So without
further delay, let me explain the contest rules. This contest as you
know is a new and novel one. In order to win, you must dance your
damnedest; a genre of dance that I dare not elaborate upon. Perhaps,
if only to add; that if you are an accomplished ballroom dancer, can
glissade with ease over pebbled blacktop, or regularly attended
Irish wakes or Italian weddings…you don't stand a chance of winning.
I'd tell you to go home, but listen to that wind out there. Sounds like
Hurricane Bruce is blowing to beat the band. Les, hope you don't mind
a little competition. So you really good dancers...you may as well stay
for the hurricane party. Looks like no one will be going home early tonight.
So, to get on with it lads and lassies, this is how it goes. There will be
three elimination heats.

The first is the slow dance set. Three slow dance tunes will be performed
by BSR, and the dancers are to dance all three unless asked to leave the
dance floor by an official escort. All styles of slow dance will be permitted.

The best advice for you to follow is...no running. Walk...or Stroll. A slow Cha-cha or rumba is okay, but slow it down speed freaks.

The second dance set will consist of three numbers with the pick-up pace of Southern California Country Rock, and the 60s and 70s tempo set to Doo Wop, Soul Jazz and the Twist.
Dancers, its open season. You may dance the, Watusi, Mashed Potato, the Twist, Cool Jerk, Swim, Hand Jive, Booga Loo, Hop, Bunny, Pony and the Bird. But remember, allegretto boys and girls. Not so slow, and not so fast.

And the third and final three dance numbers will be the Jump Blues, Hip Hop, Swing and Jitterbug at Indi pace. In other words...You can let 'er rip. For those of you who make it this far into the contest? Well may Terpsichore the Greek muse of dance be with you. May the winners' joint replacement surgeries be successful and their physical therapy brief.

As for the judges scoring, listen up and take notes. It is the best of the worst that scores in this race for the crown. The faut pas plenty, and the folie a deux dance duo collects the purse. Here's how:

SCORE ITEM	POINTS
Brief Nudity (1 sec. or less)	10
Male Lead Abdication with Collision	10
With Injury	15
Dancing Alone while Partner Disoriented or Unconscious (less than 30 sec.)	20
Partner's Both Feet off the Floor (more than 3 sec.)	15
Both Partners' Two Feet off the Floor (No time limit)	25
Ordinary Falls (No Pratt falls. The judges know a real klutz when they see one)	10
Dancing with a Compound Fracture	50
Dancing with your Imaginary Friend	25
Dancing with Your Partner's Imaginary Friend	25
Dancing with a Stationary Object (that isn't your partner)	20
Dancing to Your Own Drummer	0
Dancing Well- Instant Elimination	-100

The first couple to score 100 points or more is the winner. In the event of a tie, the dancers will exchange partners. The couple who conforms to the dance form of the music being played and yet dances it most poorly will be declared the winner. It is very likely that this will be a dance to the death (literally), because the chances of this happening are staggering.

Causes for Elimination: If it is found out - and these Serbs have ways of finding out that would shock you, literally - that: you have received a certificate of successful completion from a school of dance; have been raised by Black sharecroppers, your Puerto Rican mother and sisters, or in an Italian neighborhood in Philadelphia, <u>or</u> on an Indian reservation; *or, last but not least,* attended your high school prom and participated - you will be instantly disqualified, remanded into the custody of SMOG and sent to the Croatian Dance Re-Education Sanatorium. Anyone who knows that he or she has entered under false pretenses...may sign up for the amnesty program and be forgiven after your whipping. Hey, lighten up square dancers. Just kidd 'n.

Now let the contest begin. Wow, listen to that storm out there. Hey, Les, better crank up the volume, and put on your rubber sole shoes. Everyone with a number, come out here on the dance floor. Judges, are you ready? [The judges nod, 'yes']. Les, 'a one and a two and a three.' Yowza! Yowza! Yowza! [Les begins with a slow dance. The couples take a minute or more to pair up, figure out which hand gets held and which is placed on the small of the back]. More difficult, it appears, is with which foot to begin?

"#9. The next proposed area of research is possibly the most subtle and the most difficult to pursue. It concerns two sets of interrelated dichotomies: slow/fast dancers and soft touch/hard touch dancers...I proposed the possibility that dancers who tended to move slowly would generally be heavier than dancers who move quickly...I speculate whether dancers who have the "soft touch", i.e., who tend to use a light dynamic through most of their dancing, would have a characteristic injury pattern, and, conversely, whether dancers whose movement is pervaded by the "hard touch," i.e., a continually forceful style, would have a different injury pattern."

From, <u>How to Dance Forever</u>
<u>Surviving Against The Odds</u>
By, Daniel Nagrin

Daniel, sir, I have collected so much data for your research proposals that I insist on being placed on your payroll and sent monthly checks. Better yet, I'm in the process of having my accountant - who doubles as my bodyguard - establish a charitable trust fund to be used for the rehabilitation of injured dancers. So in lieu of a monthly check directly deposited into my personal bank account, make a donation to the Stuart Dance Re-education Sanatorium. This is where the casualties of the Millennium Dance Contest will be living out their remaining, tortured years adapting to their prosthetic devices, receiving neurological rehab for gait training, and taking daily dance instruction from the staff of SMOG Physical Therapy, Inc. I'm getting ahead of myself. Just like I did during the slow dance set with Eve.

Eve danced superbly which really screwed me up. I insisted on taking the lead, once, twice... again. She resisted my every effort to guide her through those simple one-two, one-two steps.

I once regarded the slow dance as relatively safe. Safe enough so that any man who'd ordinarily decline a dance invitation was willing to allow himself a slow dance with his date. And you've seen how weak an effort this act requires: shuffle your date to the dance floor; Velcro her to your chest; and rock back-and-forth till the music stops, or until she falls asleep. Eve's tiny geisha girl steps are what always throw me off. She feels as though she competing in the broad jump when we slow dance together. My four feet, six inch stride is a hazard to Eve as well as the other dancers. Like I were driving a logging truck without brakes and fish tailing around the bend on a wet mountain road. Look out partner. Here I come! Eve was dragged on the undercarriage of my scissor-moves for about ten feet before I collided with Grace and Ben. Actually, more with Grace than with Ben. I got Grace on her protruding hip as she was about to dip Ben. I may as well have dove head first into a plow share. Grace shook me and Eve off with about as much finesse as she'd have used to flick entangled love bugs off her windshield. Grace was unstoppable on the dance floor. Unfortunately, I, Eve and Ben were not. Worse than any bone or muscle injury - or to our pride - was that we scored points! We would be eligible for the next dance set. We would not be among the chosen concentration camp inmates to be mercifully dispatched. Eve, who on any other Friday night, would have been ecstatic that I had offered my hand and walked her to the waxed floor of slip and slide to dance...was livid. I had for the first time in all of my dancing days, few as they may be, had a woman angry with me for keeping up with the competition. I envied the dancers who were tapped on the shoulder and led off the dance floor by SMOG escorts. Peculiar as it may seem, none of those losers had walked off with their heads hung in shame. Their smugness was nauseating. This phenomenon was most striking with the couple I had barely recognized as the Venezuelas. They were disguised as Ashley regulars. If they had arrived in stretch pants with Theresa in her elastic halter top, I'd have instantly recognized them. But they had infiltrated the contest like yuppie commandos planning an Amway party. They had tried to pass themselves off as Target fashion models. They almost passed, and would have; had Johnnie not gotten his confidence back. He and Theresa swept through those slow dances unlike any drop-in-price special. All eyes were on them. Their movements...flawless. They were caught. I waved to Johnnie and Theresa bye-bye style. Johnnie cupped his hands around his mouth and shouted as he was being pulled roughly off the floor, "Hey Stew (I hate it when anyone calls me that), it took me awhile to get over that bug. I'm much, much better now." The bastard had to rub it in. I was sure Eve felt the same way.

It was small consolation that a few of my best friends had survived the first heat. Bob and Claire were still standing. I can't figure out how they scored. It must have been Bob's creative form, and the moves that are his trademark that impressed the judges. Bob parried like a fencer, fluttered like a butterfly and Cossack-danced like a midget on roller skates. At the end of each number he bowed to Claire like royalty. The Serbs mistook him for the Prince of Kosovo. Claire really ate up the royal treatment. She and Bob weren't ones to complain, like me, about moving on to the next event. In fact I think Bob was looking forward to dancing in that sector of the dance floor that he and Claire shared with Carmen Maria Esmeralda Silverstein, a.k.a., Kelly Le Brock. I knew that it wasn't coincidence that Bob dropped to a seated position and danced Cassock-style to a Maria Cary song while Carmen scored three times for brief nudity. Bob didn't know I was on to him. I know him, and he's inclined to pull cheap stunts like that. Eve wouldn't believe me when I told her that Bob bears watching, and that someone should have policed his actions. Eve twists things around. "Stew (urgh!), Bob needs no help watching what's bare. He seems quite flexible. And besides, I suspect those SMOG goons have had plenty of police experience. I don't think they need any help from you. And...maybe if you were paying more attention to me, my knees would have skin on them and I'd still be wearing panty hose, and you, Stew (ouch!), would be enjoying a better view from the seating section." 'Eve, Eve, Eve,' I was wise enough to say only to myself.

    SMOG officials kept us corralled like Albanians at a Mac Donald's open house. Packed in and hungry for more. I'm not particularly eager to tell you what happened next. Well, I'm here aren't I? Writing about what happened means at least...I survived.

I did try to get Eve and I eliminated. I also knew that it was entirely up to me, and that I couldn't count on Eve to dance *well enough* for the both of us and get us disqualified.

In addition to reading, <u>Shall We Dance,</u> by Manine Golden, and following the footprint cutouts that help you with position, heal and toe placement, and direction, I had gone above and beyond the call of stupidity. I let Eve lure me into this mess. I practiced; when no one was around of course.

I might have been a bit more open to critique. I could have counted on Angie's and Zack's brutal honesty concerning my solitary dance interludes. I just couldn't humble myself to accept the constructive criticism from my kids. My movie habits made me afraid to trust them. Would you trust the advice of a Linda Blair and Damian look-a-like? I'll take my chances when I'm a grand-father. So what did I do? I resorted to Unity Church gimmicks. Okay, so I was desperate. And I never applied these more vigorously than in preparation for the second heat. The one with the pick-up pace of Southern California Country Rock. I *'visualized'* dancing like a pro. Dan Nagrin must belong to Unity too. Because he sneaked this visualization idea into his book in his doctor bashing chapter (he must be insured by an HMO), "Healers and Treatments." He gives a tentative endorsement for *ideokinesis*. It should have read *idiot*kinesis. By the end of the contest, I had had plenty of practice with both.

With ideokinesis you are your own guru. This is a dangerous practice in and of itself. The initiate's climb to the mountaintop to commune with the guru is a journey fraught with hazards. For most of us such a difficult and time consuming journey isn't efficient, cost effective or covered by insurance. Most companies begrudge a three-hour training block, but they'll buy the idea if the Industrial gurus will guarantee greater productivity and a Japanese obsequiousness to the company papa san. You're saying, what has this to do with dance or *this* dance contest? It has a lot to do with it. Because I didn't have time to practice all that much. What I needed was a supplement to boost my minimum daily requirement of dance practice. Even I had to admit that two weeks wasn't enough to become a Met performer. I didn't have the three or four weeks that I knew it would take for all of those complex routines to coalesce into Balanchine virtuosity on the dance floor. And I couldn't renew the library book that I checked out on the topic because there were too many people on the waiting list. So I reached out. Way out, and read about ideokinesis before I went to bed Thursday night. It was the very miracle I had been praying for.

IDEOKINESIS

This is a staggeringly brilliant concept developed out of the theories of Mabel Elsworth Todd, who wrote a book called *The Thinking Body*...The briefest compression of this complexity is one that should be familiar to most dancers. It states that the concepts that exist in the mind about the body, its structure and its motions, are fundamentally what determine our alignment and motion. By mentally clarifying the actual structure and functioning of a well body and learning to image these, a repatterning is supposed to take place...I believe Ideokinesis is worthy of the most extravagant research efforts. It says if you have the right concept, idea and/or poem of the motion, the motion will be right. Isn't this the way most of us work in the classroom, in the rehearsal hall and onstage?"

From, <u>How To dance Forever</u>
By, Daniel Nagrin

Can you image my excitement when I chanced upon this miraculous encounter with the never- before- revealed secrets of the great dancers. 'I couldn't sleep all last night' (Bobby Darin)...I lay tossing and turning, turning and tossing'...as I imagined dancing the night away. Damn if I didn't wake up exhausted Friday morning. Then, after working all day, I was in no shape to dance competitively. Eve said that my complaining about being tired was the cop out of a coward. She's very competitive when it comes to a tired match. She uses her fatigue athletically. Because, 'no matter how sleepy,' I've heard her say, 'I can always bring myself to dance...because I love to dance.' She swears that it revitalizes her. Weariness, on the other hand, makes me clumsy. Which probably explains why I tripped over Eve so easily when Grace swung her hip in our path.

Eve assumed that because my eyes were closed before the fast set began that I was dozing on my feet. The truth was...I was visualizing dancing like the All-American-Bandstand boy that my mother had hoped I'd become when she took me to that dance studio in Philadelphia. Upon reflecting on the Freudian implications in this brief reverie brought on , no doubt, by fatigue, I shifted to imagining myself dancing in a way that would make Eve so proud that she'd let me lead. Relieved that my powerful imagination wouldn't snap me back to awareness with my pre-teen acne, and a Waveset pompadour, I visualized moving with caballero coolness. My hunch is that a lot of people use ideokinesis and don't realize they are doing it. You hear music on the radio, you close your eyes, and you see yourself dancing, 'dancing like you've never danced before.' *Flash Dance*, right? Never a lesson, yet there you are in the body electric (sometimes naked); coordinated, animated and graceful beyond belief... in your mind's eye of course. I've leapt, cart wheeled, done the split and danced the night away in the imaginary safety of the dance-studio-in-my-mind. And here was Dan telling me that all it takes to dance like a pro and overcome the real hazards of the dance floor at the Ashley is to form the right concept. All I had to do was compose a 'poem of motion,' and the motion would be right! I had the good sense to interpolate that the poem should be Whitmanesque – 'I Dance the Body Electric,' instead of something from, say, Poe or The Jerky Boys. I was on the eighth stanza of my mental dance poem [being drilled by Sister Yolanda in meter counts and proper verse form while I danced to the bells, the sticks, the triangle and the tambourine] when I heard Eve shouting at me, "Stewart, are you going to dance, or are you going to just stand there rolling your head around and acting like Stevie Wonder. We've already scored 20 points for *Dancing with Your Disoriented Partner*. "Good going Stewart!" Shit! This ideokinesis is powerful stuff. And I thought acid was wild. It was Eve's quick thinking and her paying attention to her dance partner for a change that brought me back just in time so that she wouldn't score another point for dancing well without me. I was alert. Oriented to the structure of the music and its prescribed motions. I was at last properly aligned and in motion. I heard BSR playing Iggy Pop. I visualized that I was Eve's 10 for 10 computer-matched dance-partner. I was Antonio Banderas. She was Melanie Griffith. I held my arms high, clapped my hands to the torrid beat. My clapping hands echoed in perfect timing with the racing heart within Melan... Eve's breast. My feet moved with the rhythmic speed of a Harlem tap dancer. My hips and Eve's moved in syncopated harmony. We were in love with the dance. We and the music and the dance were...ONE! We were immediately eliminated. Eve was dragged from the dance floor. She kicked and blocked the SMOG escort's advances, but she was no match against the both of us. Eve doesn't like the taste of defeat, particularly for the wrong reasons. She fell silent as we stood among the spectators. She realized that she would never dance with Antonio again. Chocolate covered Prozac wouldn't have snapped her out of that mood. She was a foot from the summit of K-2, with the national flag in her outstretched hand, when she was prematurely bucketed away by rescue helicopter against her will.

It was in the quiet moment following our defeat that we finally took notice of the storm. The wind's pitch had intensified. Bruce was blowing to beat the band. Les reacted to the shrill keening of the big blow as if it were a background noise to be dealt with; in the way that musicians typically do. By increasing volume and reverb. More bass, extra tweeter and wide open horn. For Les and Bruce the competition had only just begun. Les belted out a song that rocked the house; signaling that the second fast set number had begun. The tail-end crowd closest to the doors and windows moved toward the center of the bar, casting cautious glances behind them in anticipation of being startled by an unwelcome visitor that was about to burst through the doors and climb their backs like an alley cat. Those daring to remain close to the exits shivered with a chill produced by the cooling of perspiration under damp polyester. Wind whistled through the gaps around doors and windows.

The air inside the Ashley was charged with fear and excitement. Different from the usual trepidation associated with mingling and dancing on other Friday nights at the Ashley. I considered leaving and making a dash to safer shelter. I suggested this to Eve whose funk had deepened into existential dread with a touch of mania. "What? Leave now and miss all the fun. What's the matter, Stew? A little storm scares you? Face your fears. Stay. Dance!" She had done it. Eve tore at my defenses. She psychologically de-pantsed me in public and exposed my fears. I hadn't fooled her with my false bravado when I retorted loud enough to be heard over the noise of the band, "Hey, Eve, let's go rent an ultra-light and catch a bitchin updraft." Meaning, 'Let's go over to the Baptist church on West Ocean Boulevard. It's a designated storm shelter.' I was there to stay. With Eve taking charge as always...and leading us both into such peril I couldn't know for sure.

Les really pitched to the crowd with the second fast-dance selection. He couldn't have picked more apt song titles. BSR played a Les-crafted medley of *Deliverance* and *Clean My Wounds* by Corrosion of Conformity. He rounded off the set with *Waste of Mind* by Zebra Head. The crowd majorly identified. It must have taken many back to the cradle when they were rocked to the 8-track lullabies of Ozzie Osborn and Alice Cooper. Here was a crowd that needed Dramamine to stave off dance-induced motion sickness, and hockey equipment to prevent injuries. They should have stopped at Walgreens and The Sports Authority before they walked through the doors of the Ashley. Couples danced with reckless abandon, and scored with unintended vengeance. I was reminded of the bumper cars at the amusement park. A ride I liked as a kid. Thrilled by rubber bumpered, mini-cars accelerating over polished metal floors. Intrigued by the steel whip brushing the voltage charged ceiling. Hearing the snap and the crackle of electricity. Inhaling the ozone and the axle grease. Feeling the dry rain of carbon particles showering down on me from the ceiling, and then...suddenly, meeting another car in head-on, side-on, and in rear-end collisions. It was a childhood recollection enhanced by Darla's approach. She was approaching the quadrant of the dance floor from which Eve and I were observing the action. It was the fastest I had ever seen Darla move. She must have been propelled by breezes that wafted through the windows, doors and straining rafters of the old building. She spirited over the polished floor, light as an apparition.

From the far corner of the dance floor, her partner sped toward her like a spinning top. He intercepted her at a dead stop. Both gazed into each other's eyes. A moment passed. Their dark, lifeless eyes met. A signal was exchanged in a look and a nod that communicated their next move. In the blink of an eye, they launched into a pirouette like figure skaters on ice and locked in an embrace. Like a shot, they broke away in opposite directions like Tasmanian devils in pursuit of separate prey. The smell of sulfur - and I dare say, axle grease - trailed in their wake (no pun). Ash rained down on us as they sped past. They suddenly froze as if snared. Immobilized before the crucifixes worn by quick moving SMOG Officials who escorted Darla and her date from the dance floor. An astute Serbian SMOG nationalist recognized their dance as the pavane, a 16th Century dance of the royal courts. Darla's 78 rpm version didn't fool those Transylvania Serbs. Darla's real undoing was having found the Mr. Somebody in the Number 1 Jersey. She must have freed him from that locker in time for the contest. He must have been in there for a very, very long time. He was probably just expressing his gratitude when he accepted her invitation to be her partner in the contest.

The field of competition wasn't narrowing by any significant margin. Bayou Bonnie and J.R., who had danced the earlier, slow dance set like champions of the Ashley, were eliminated shortly after Darla and her date were carried off by their SMOG pallbearers. My guess was that Bayou Bonnie and J.R. were captivated by their spell. A transformation occurred that was coincidental with their having gazed too long on the pavane. Maybe the power of the spell was in having witnessed a dance danced well. Or...maybe it was a conjuring of the back-woods Louisiana spirit that set Bayou Bonnie's and J.R.'s rhythms right. The milonga and the Cajun hipitty-hop polka beat entered their high healed Justins and made them dance-literate. J.R. scored once when he lifted his little Bonnie off the floor for the count of thirty. The judges refused to count it because Bayou Bonnie was still dancing in the air, and doing it...too well. A burley, muscle-packed escort grabbed her. She was still dancing in mid-air - arms waving, head shaking and feet stomping - like a live crawdad on a hot skillet - as they carried her away. J.R., on the other hand, tucked himself into a compact ball, and clamped his strong, smithy arms around knees fat as cypress stumps, when he saw the escorts coming for him. He fought like an armadillo and was just as difficult to hang onto. The escorts called for reinforcements. I heard Bayou Bonnie's adenoids burst as she cried, "Fowl." The volume of her nasal Louisiana drawl exceeded the decibel range of the raging storm.

After Bayou Bonnie and J.R.'s ousting, Buhl was eliminated. Buhl had always danced alone at the Ashley, usually clinging to a pillar for company. Rumor had it that Buhl had a jealous underage girlfriend, and because of her tender (not legal) years, she could not accompany him to the adult-only dance contest. Word travels fast in Stuart. And if Buhl was seen dancing with another woman - or girl as the case may be - female spies in the employ of Buhl's girlfriend would report it to her, and Buhl would be seriously hurting before sunrise the next day. Buhl entered the Millennium Dance Contest under false pretenses. He claimed he had a partner, and when he arrived only with his cousin Butch, well, people assumed that he and his 'cous were a thing. You know, gay. What, with the matching leather shorts, physiques by Andro and drivers licenses with Okeechobee addresses, well, what would you think. Only the SMOG men seemed to disapprove. They treated David Morgan and Charlie in the same rude manner. But when they snarled at Buhl, Buhl lunged at them, and put bouncers, Serges and Petro, in a head lock that induced mild asphyxia, strained ligaments, and gained respect. And Butch wasn't even the solitary dancer type. He just stared with evil malice at any SMOG shirt that came anywhere near him. Buhl had danced the slow dance set within arm's reach of Butch who stayed glued to the floor amidst the first row of spectators. Buhl scored heavily during the first set for *Dancing with a Stationary Object* [with Butch who either was or wasn't his partner], and got away with it because no SMOG escort would dare to approach him. At least not until they were x-rayed and medically cleared to return to bouncing for a living. At the start of the fast set, Buhl slowed to a shuffle. He hunkered down. Reached into his pants pockets, and pulled out four glow sticks; two in each hand. He danced an erratic jig while he tore open the wrappers with his teeth. He snapped them in half to disperse the chemicals that produced their glow. They came to life and light and so did Buhl. Buhl danced like a bull frog in a fire fly swarm. He leapt like *The Notorious Jumping Frog of Calaveras County*. He'd have made Lionidas W. Smiley and Dan Nagrin proud. Substitute Lionidas' exclamatory, 'Flies, Dan'l, flies!' with 'Flies, Buhl, flies!' and you've got the picture.

"Yet when we jump, leap, or run, our entire weight of over one hundred pounds [add an extra hundred for Buhl] crashes into the hard surface of a floor or lands like a whisper. The complex mass of responses and moves that make it possible for a trained dancer to land on his "bag of bones" without a sound or perceptible hit is one of the central miracles of good dance training and nowhere as common as it should be...It's a lifesaver when you have it and a destructive flaw when you don't. Consistent traumatic shocks will in all probability contribute to every structural weakness from your anklebone right up to your head bone."

From, How to Dance Forever

By, Daniel Nagrin

Old Buhl, eyes closed, danced off the floor, out the doors, onto Main Street and into the on-coming headlights of an F-250 on 6-inch suspension lifts hauling ass on 44-inch Groundhawgs in search of the nearest hurricane evacuation route. Buhl dove like a glow-stick crazed Raver into the maul of fancy grillwork, high beams and a rebel-call horn. Ralph's shout, in his Slovak mother-language, betrayed his liability anxiety. Above the roar of wind and driving rain, he yelled, *"Pozovite hola zu hitme pomoc."* Eve asked the smiling Serges what it meant. Serges, lacking genuine concern for the injured Buhl, translated..."It means, call a fucking ambulance," after which he displayed the poor taste of bursting into laughter. Buhl scored nonetheless, but he was out of the contest. His attempt to dance with fading glow sticks, double vision and multiple, compound fractures was judged as incomplete when he passed out a mere few inches short of making it back to the dance floor. Buhl was tough. He'd survive his injuries. His underage girlfriend had put him through a lot worse.

So the floor was still packed with contestants when the third and final set began. Les' metronome for the Jump Blues, Hip Hop, Swing and Jitterbug sequence was set at max range on the digital quartz oscillator built into his heart pace maker. He drank liquid nitro straight from the bottle, quivered in readiness, and played the classic rift that sends out the hounds to chase the fox. Hurricane Bruce was beginning to gain on BSR, and he threatened to drown them out in both sound and storm surge.

By the third set, Hurricane Bruce had arrived. And the storm was no longer one which could be ignored. Bruce begged for attention like a disturbed teenager whose noisy and destructive behavior is driven by poltergeist forces. Bruce wrapped on windows, banged on doors and howled like a banshee. Les blew a speaker trying to compete.

Dismembered palm fronds charged at windows and hung wet and suspended by gale force winds. Pets scurrying for cover were propelled down Main Street like white-eyed tumbleweed deprived of their motor control. Hoss and the kitchen help barricaded the front doors with a board that they nailed in place with six-penny nails. It felt as though the storm was about to plow right through the building. Eve's fantasy was that we were in a sequel to the movie, 'Titanic.' Movie, bad dream, raging storm? Didn't matter what you called it. We were living it now. It would end the same. Yet just the same, the band played on.

Les rode the brown outs, the power surges and the dance contestant knock-outs like a cabby careening through the pot-holed streets of New York City. Les was unperturbed. He possessed Zen master single-pointedness, and no disaster, fickle act of nature or nitro-induced Shiva- hallucinated vision of world annihilation was going to sway him from his purpose. Which was to play the music to the dance-to-the-death, better known as the Millennium Dance Contest.

BSR was cook'n. The dancers had more important things to worry about than a Class 5 Hurricane. They had to survive the next three numbers. They'd apply for federal disaster relief tomorrow, if they made it through the night. Les took his cue from Ozzie on bass, who suggested an old number by Fishbones called, *Party at Ground Zero*. It must have been Ozzie's view from stage that inspired the selection.

Ozzie must have had a premonition of what was about to happen on that little dance floor crowded with...dancers, whose pent-up energies were about to be unleashed. He must have foreseen the explosion of limbs that the music and the power of Hurricane

Bruce were about to ignite. It was a fact that it was way too small a space into which to cram such an enormous amount of nervous energy.

> "7. The Dance Space: ...If you must work on a dangerous surface, go over the choreography carefully to see whether you can modify falls and aerial work so that you and/or your dancers don't live to remember that day with bitterness. Use kneepads and padding whenever possible, and if costuming does not permit it, at least use them for rehearsals. Many of the best-equipped studios have inadequate space for dancers. Avoid them if you can, and try to have equipment brought to a proper dance space."
>
> From: <u>How to Dance Forever</u>
> By, Daniel Nagrin

That explains the fleet of ambulances parked behind the Ashley. Hearses would have been more appropriate, but Hoss and Annie erred on the side of showing better taste and by adhering to industry standards. They chose the medical readiness protocol for of a rugby match, or a Boston Bruins game, or a bull fight. They might have saved more lives if they had set up a mash unit, and used the kitchen as an operating theater. You think I'm being morbid; exaggerating the dance handicaps of the contestants to make them out to be more of a danger to themselves and others than they actually deserve. Well you weren't there. Take my word for it. I have actually been understating the menace that they represented. These were no ordinary people to begin with.

No ordinary dancers, they. These were not Dan's people. The Ashley seppuku dancers were not destined to dance forever. Their destiny was something far greater, or far graver, depending on your point of view. Although you might have already guessed it by their over-the-top performance, and the way they threw themselves into the fast dance set…on that oh so fateful evening. Oh, yes! Les *wailed*. No one, and I mean no one, could not, not dance to the contagious, foot-tapping, hand-clapping music of BSR. You catch Swing faster than a spit ball coming at your eye. *Party at Ground Zero* initiated a melt-down of the entire crowds' dance inhibitions. Adrenals were super heating; central nervous systems had reached a dangerous state of fast-twitch overload. And Bruce was getting ready to join BSR on stage, and accompany Les and the band in the finale.

And then it all happened so suddenly. I know what a barrel-assing electron must feel like when it collides with a nucleus traveling in the opposite direction in the Hadrons particle accelerator. What happened at the Ashley happened in a cyclotron of sorts created by a combination of events. A virtual cyclotron, or at least like the one they bring to the Martin County Fair ever year. Where you spin faster, and faster, and faster, until you're pinned to the wall and held there by centrifugal forces. Powerful forces that keep you from throwing up. Because if it weren't for the increased forces of gravity, you and everyone else sharing the same spin cycle 'd have already plastered the walls with your lunch.

I can't honestly say that Eve was the one who started it, but she was one of the instigators. Blame it on BSR, Les and the hurricane if it suits you. But Eve started gyrating her hips to the music of *Cherry Popping Daddies*. Her hip gyrations are cute when the ark of her pelvic rotations are smooth and subtle like when a woman sways to the gentle seductions of a Julio Iglesias song. But Eve began to swivel; the ark of her swing growing wider, and wider. She started wagging that little prehensile tail we humans call a tail bone. She did little jerky walking motions toward the dance floor. Eve caught me by the arm as she started making her move. I tried to shake free of her grip. It was no use. She was picking up momentum despite the fact that she had my two-hundred pounds of resistance as a drag anchor. I reminded Eve that she and I had been disqualified, and that we had no business being on the dance floor. She ignored the fact that we had no official status in the contest. Eve was responding to her sick urges. She was in full-blown relapse. The music, the dancers, the contest, the super-attenuated electric vibes…all…triggered her addiction to dance. She *made* me her dance partner. She intended to take me down with her. I implored her to just 'say no' to her urges. I sympathized, and told her that ideokinetically I knew where she was coming from, understood what she was feeling — to no avail. Rationalizing with her was useless. Where Eve was coming from, it was all irrelevant.

It was where she was going - and to where she was taking *us* - that scared the living shit out of me. And she wasn't alone. She was being followed by a procession of dance zombies. Scores of observers, disqualified contestants, volunteers and employees of the Ashley were hip-hopping and skipping to Brian Setzer's, *Dirty Boogie*.

"Swing is a modified, more sophisticated version of the jitterbug. Swing rhythm fits eight steps into six beats of music in 4/4 time. The "one and" and the "three and" beats fit into the counts of "one" and "three," respectively. The side steps should be taken with bent knees and a bounce. When stepping backward on the seventh count, be careful not to pull too far away from your partner. Remember to use the ball of your foot to step backward instead of your heel. The leader's left hand and follower's right hand drop to waist level for this dance, and partners should stand one-half foot to one foot apart in the closed hold."

From, Shall We Dance?

By, Manine Rosa Golden

Eve's dash to the dance floor wasn't intercepted. She was like a jet swooping onto the deck of an aircraft carrier. And there was no cable to catch her; not even me whose heels were dragging the floor and burning leather. She revved up and launched into a high-kick'n' jitterbug. I was caught in her iron grip; dancing in tandem against my will. Being jerked this way and that. Being spun like a top, and used for Eve's pole vaulting leaps. Then I saw Reverent Jack coming up fast. He was entering Eve's orbit. He was an interloper; a maverick asteroid. Eve launched a first strike offensive. She took out Reverend Jack who was shouting curses at Eve and me for crashing the contest. She took him out with a round house kick that Sensei Alvin Ailey would have been proud of. Jack collapsed in an ill dignified heap of twisted limbs, muttering, "Gawd Bluss

Ameriga" in a puddle of drool. His partner, Nancy Schmidt, stared at Eve. Her hard stare melted into the deep character lines and the thin smile that I had seen in paintings of Joan of Ark. Nancy looked at the fallen Jack, drove her heal into his ribs, bent over and ripped the donkey pin from his lapel and ran off the dance floor waving it over her head like a bloody scalp. "Yo, no love lost there, eh, Eve," I said. "Can we leave now?" To which Eve, executing a flying leg kick that missed my left ear by a hair's breadth, shouted, "Relax, will you? Loosen up and dance." The closest I came to dancing was to weave, dodge and duck in self-defense. From both her and the flying objects that sailed through the Ashley when Hurricane Bruce flung open the door and joined in the fray.

Bruce rushed us like Bruce of Scotland intent upon beating the powder out of the curly wigs. Street grit, rain and debris blew in on the crowd. A few solid objects traveling too fast to identify sailed through the seating section and landed in the food prep area. They landed with such a racket that the kitchen staff let out startled screams. Sheet music burst from a music stand. A dozen wigs and hairpieces were snatched from the heads of contestants. Another gust sent them flying at the spectators. A Hitchcock trauma was re-lived as people waved their hands wildly at the air to drive off what suddenly became homicidal sea gulls flocking to Stuart from Bodega Bay. Les was furious. He hated competition [noise and mayhem] from any other source than himself and BSR. Les dug in. He was losing electrical power but he wouldn't lose the battle of the bands. This was how Les regarded the storm; as a competitor. He had turned it into a grudge match. Les obviously relished power struggles. Mixing metaphors would do him in. This was bad weather, not Tolstoy. Nevertheless, Les picked up a handful of six-penny nails that were ripped from the ply-wood barricades. He raised his microphone like the Hammer of Thor, and nailed his boots to the stage. He leaned into the wind, now gusting through the Ashley at a stiff eighty knots. Les threatened to shoot any band member who tried to desert. He stood fast, and played. We moved. It was difficult to distinguish dance from just not being able to stand still. BSR never missed a note.

The band was gaining. So was the hurricane. *Everyone* was in motion. The judges couldn't stay in their chairs. The angels left their pedestals. I was startled to observe their absence. I nudged Eve toward the kitchen. It worked. She mistook my tact to safe harbor as an attempt to lead. So I took advantage of Eve for being so gullible. She must have thought, 'Stewart has finally come around. He's let go. He's dancing…*with* me. I don't care if it's the alcohol or male menopause…he's dancing!' I closed my eyes. I prayed that my memory wouldn't fail me. Coordination was another kind of problem I didn't want to think about. I have a good memory. I photographed Manine's Swing diagram and filed it in my brain's hard drive. And just in case I forgot, I printed it out at home, and put it in my pants pocket before I left the house. I discretely withdrew it, held it in the palm of my hand behind Eve's right shoulder, drew her into the closed hold so that she couldn't see me cheating and concentrated like my life depended on it. Because it did.

(PICTURE)

1. Left foot to side.		One
2. Right foot closes to left foot	And	
3. Left foot to side		Two
4. Right foot steps in place		Three
5. Left foot closes to right foot	And	
6. Right foot to side		Four
7. Left foot back		Five
8. Right foot in place		Six

This routine moved me in the direction of the kitchen. I knew it would be safer there. A tail wind of, now, eighty-five knots helped. If we had capsized in an ocean liner and were adrift in the Gulf Stream without life jackets, Eve wouldn't have been any more concerned. Hell, she was dancing. Nothing else mattered. Now, others were beginning to panic. They couldn't put all their efforts into trying to dance. So all of a sudden a lot of other things began to matter - like survival, surfing the big ones, finding a hurricane party or stowing away on an ark – choosing which option being influenced by I.Q., personality type and religious affiliation.

I caught sight of Charlie McQueen, David Morgan and his crew making their way to the doors. David was leading the way, his kilt blown up...argh...like an umbrella turned inside out by the wind. It concealed his tartan sash and purse, nothing else. A rude updraft revealed his arse, his Betty Boop tattoo and his umbrella latch. And Eve, who if shipwrecked, wouldn't feel put out by having to tread water for days (just as long as she could do it to music playing on her floating, battery-powered radio) commented, "They're fools if they plan to leave on Charlie's sloop." I, on the other hand, didn't comment at all. I needed to stay focused. I pretended to be Stewart, the Born Again Dervish. I would stay and take my chances among the pots and pans.

Eve and I were making good progress, and I had nearly danced her into the kitchen, when we were stopped in coordinated mid-kick, by Belisarius Jones. You may remember him as the clothes horse of the Army and Navy Outlet's, Gentlemen's Quarterly. The dude with the 2/4 fade, tribal tattoos and the baseball cap with the crown shaped like an orange carp. Well Belisarius was galloping at full speed, pounding his temples, covered with sweat and foaming at the bridle. Belisarius was obviously smitten with *grisi siknis*. I had seen this rare disorder only once before, when I visited a UNISEF clinic in Nicaragua in 1973. A Miskito native had it. He complained of headache, anxiety and fear. He had been running aimlessly for days before his comrades brought him down with a well-aimed curare dart. Well, poor Belisarius. Who could blame him? The chaos surrounding him had entered him like a bad spirit. Belisarius was probably living here on a forged green card. He left the Ashley at full throttle, bucking a head wind of eighty-five knots, pursued by the hallucinated hounds of the INS, the CIA, the ATF, the NSA, the FBI and SMOG.

It took me a confused minute or two to get my bearings, and figure out where I left off on the dance schematic. Soon we were off again. Familiar faces and limbs flew by us in a blur. I immediately recognized Carmen's full, firm and unwrinkled derri... red dress. She blew by. Red sails unfurled and full of wind. Her stern rising and falling as she swept by unsteadily on Latin platform pumps strapped to her dainty ankles. Bud (the Cassock) Toby's shock of hair preceded him. He looked like a mustang traveling in reverse with his partner Katrina riding Bud bareback. With Bud blind to what lay ahead, Katrina was no match for the bar into which Bud unintentionally steered her. Both took out the top-shelf liquors; sparing themselves the embarrassment of getting hurt on cheap booze. Had Katrina been coherent at the time, she might have felt ashamed about the scarlet letter "A" bar emblem that stuck to her bare breasts and clung there in a sticky, syrupy coating of Grenadine and maraschino cherries. That fancy font plastic "A" always intrigued me. That it stood for *Ashley* was a fact I had taken for granted.

I don't recall what happened to anyone else after Bud and Katrina ate the bar. I danced Eve into the vestibule of the kitchen where things were calmer if no less noisy. I could have sworn I heard BSR playing *So, So Def Bass* stridently and off key in defiance of Bruce. It might have been Bruce playing solo. The fate of Les remains a mystery.

So does the fate of all but the worst dancers. I don't know what happened to the best dancers. The best of the worst had danced themselves into this same safe corner, into which I corralled Eve. It was there in the kitchen that we waited it out - through the brief calm of the eye of the storm, and then through the encore return and finally the tempest's quiet ending. If it weren't for me, Eve would be listed among the missing. I don't expect any expression of gratitude from her. If we were the last two remaining people on earth, living in the Garden of Paradise, rent free, and having big backyard picnics like in the Publix commercials, she'd stay pissed because she'd have only have me to dance with. All of the good dancers would not yet be born, and only then would they have a less than 50:50 chance of inheriting Eve's recessive dance gene. Dance-mutant genes like I and most real men have are known to be dominant. Antonio would represent the Garden of Eden's serpent. You know how the rest goes: Eve, the serpent, the offer to dance from the snake. Eve accepting. All of us being evicted. Spending week-ends at the Ashley. Genesis all over again.

And that's how the Millennium Dance Contest ended...without a winner. Left wondering, trying to imagine who'd have received the honor of being crowned the 'Best of the Worst Dancers.' We'd have to wait another thousand years to find out.

Epilogue

It is yet unknown how wide-spread was the cataclysmic storm. I know this much: most of the town's - if not the world's - good dancers had vanished. As an eye-witness I can also tell you that the Ashley dancers continue to thrive. I would dare you to go there and see for yourself. But that's not possible. It's gone. In its place is another establishment. A chain restaurant no less.

We have all settled into new or re-built homes. Life continues on. Sometime after the reconstruction, I ventured out and came upon the Ashley incarnate. Suffice it to say that I have found the scenes described in this story re-enacted every week-end in a place down along the Indian River. It is situated on the marina. I wish I could be more specific, but if I gave out the address, I would be risking being sued by the proprietors. They have made it threateningly clear that they don't want anyone bashing their customer's [in]abilities. Since the Big One, the American Disabilities Act now protects people who are dance-impaired. The country has become a huge welfare state because of successful lobbying by this group.

As for the fate of Charlie McBride, David Morgan and crew? It is rumored that they managed to board their darting little sloop. At first, they were thought to be lost after having been swept dangerously close to the Ashley when the St. Lucie River rose with the storm surge. But as it turned out, when the eye of the storm passed over, they had managed to navigate into the open waters of the Atlantic where wind and fate decided their final destination. The rest is legend. There are reports from Eastern Europe that the Croatian Dance Re-education Sanatorium is once more flourishing, and contributing generously to the arts in the name of their new icon, Dan. It has also gladdened the young fathers of the new Western Democracies that the SMOG Republic has been formed, and is spreading an appreciation of folk dances and capitalism throughout the Global Third World.

I am thankful to the heavens that Angie and Zack have returned safely to us. Since they take after me, down to their two left feet, I hadn't really feared for their survival. However, they have no idea where their grand-mother is. The kids say she was surprisingly buoyant, as the tidal surge propelled her eastward. She drifted off the coast of Cape Cod, and was last spotted heading for New Foundland.

A list of dances

How many forms of dance would you be able to name? Just off the top of your head, go ahead and list as many as you can. Write them down. Did you name a few or many. If you had to guess, how many kinds of dance style categories are there in the world? What number did you guess?

Well, there are at least five-hundred and forty-two dance categories. And this is by no means all-inclusive, and doesn't account for all that exist. The list of dances which follow is open ended, and will grow even longer as people contribute some exotic form or another that's not listed.

How many of the following dances have you learned? Are you the Jill or the Jack of many dances, and the master of ….? Or are you as clumsy as I, and the master of none.

List of dances
From Wikipedia,

This is the main list of dances. It is a non-categorized, index list of specific dances. There may also be listed dances which could either be considered a specific dance or a family of related dances, depending on your perspective. For example ballet, ballroom dance and folk dance can be considered a single dance style or a family of related dances. The purpose of the page is to have as complete an index as possible.

Specific dances are listed below in alphabetical order, and only should be listed one time. Variants of a specific dance should be listed as indented items, and not as separate items. For example Waltz has several variants. This makes the list easier to read, and avoids redundant links.

See following for categorized lists:

- List of dance style categories
- List of folk dances sorted by origin
- List of novelty/fad dances

Dances listed on these specialized (categorized) lists should also be included in this general index.

List;

A

- Acro dance
- Allemande
- Arkan (Ukrainian, Hutsul)
- Ardha (Arab tribal war dance)
- Argentine Tango
- Anaconda ([Snake Dance])
- Arial
- Attan (Pashtun)
- acharuli ([Georgian folk dance])
- azonto (Ghanaian dance)

B

- Baba Karam (Persian, Folk)
- Bachata (Latin Club, Folk)
- Balboa (Swing)
- Ballet, category, also known as classical dance
- Ballos (Burçak tarlası oyunu)(Greece), (Turkey)
- Ballroom dance, category
- Ballu tundu (Sardinia)

- Bandari dance
- Barn dance, category
- Baroque dance, category
- Barynya (Russian, folk)
- Basse danse (also Basse-dance, Bassadanse, Bassadanze. French and Italian Renaissance dances)
- Basque dance
- BBoying (Breakdance)
- Belly dance
- Beguine, dance of Caribbean origin
- Bereznianka (Ukrainian, Carpathian Ruthenia)
- Bergamask (Be dance, from Bergamo, Italy
- Bhangra (Folk Dance of Northern India)
- Bharatanatyam (Indian classical dance)
- Big Apple (Line dance)
- Bihu dance (Folk dance of Assam, India)
- Black Bottom (see Lindy Hop)
- Blues (Club dance, Swing)
- Bolero (American Ballroom, Cuban, European)
- Bollywood (Danced in Indian Movies)
- Bomba (African, Caribbean)

- Bon Odori (Japanese)
- Boogaloo
- Boogie-woogie (Swing)
- Bop, see Bop music, also ABA at List of dance organizations
- Bossa nova (Brazilian, see Bossa nova music)
- Borrowdale (Zimbabweean, see Museve music)
- Boston
- Bourrée (historical)
- Branle (Bransle) (historical)
- Breakaway (see Lindy Hop)
- Breakdancing
- Bump and grind
- Bugg
- Bunny Hop
- Butoh (Japanese)
- Butterfly (Urban, USA/Caribbean)
- Buyo (Japanese)

C

- Cat Daddy
- Cajun dance, (Louisiana, USA Regional, Cajun)

- Cajun Jig or Cajun One Step
- Cajun Jitterbug and Two Step
- Cajun Waltz
- Zydecko
- Cakewalk (Swing)
- Calypso (Caribbean)
- Candombe (Uruguayan)
- Canaries dance (historical, Renaissance, court)
- Can-can (Cancan, can can)
- Capoeira (dance and martial art, Brazilian)
- Cariñosa (dance of love) Philippines
- Carioca
- Carol (Medieval)
- Castle Walk
- Căluș (Romanian ritual dance)
- Céilidh (Ireland, Scotland and Northern England)
- Ceroc (Modern Jive, Club)
- Chacarera (Argentina)
- Chaconne
- Cha cha cha or Cha cha (Cuba, Latin Ballroom Social)
- Chamame (Chamamé, Argentina)

- Charleston
- Charmander (dance)
- Chumak (Ukrainian)
- Chasapiko (Greece)
- Cheerleading
- Chicken Dance
- Chicken Noodle Soup
- Chodzony (Poland)
- Chula (Southern Brasil)
- Cinquepace, Cinque-pace
- Circassian Dance
- Circle dance
- Clogging
- Clowning
- Cocek
- Collegiate shag
- Compas (Haiti)
- Conga
- Contact improvisation
- Contemporary dance
- Contra dance

- Cordax Greek / Roman erotic dance
- Cossack dance
- Cotillion
- Country/western dance
- Country dancing
- Country/Western Two-step
- Country Swing or Western Swing
- Courante (historical)
- Court dance
- Cueca (Chile)
- Cumbia (Colombia, Club)
- Cupid Shuffle
- Csárdás (Folk, Hungarian; also variants in Slovak dances, Rusyn dances, (Ukrainian dances, Lemko dances))
- Chowpurulia W.B. INDIA

D

- Dances of Universal Peace
- Dandia (Folk dance of Gujarat, India)
- Dabke (Levantine)
- Dilan (a Kurdish dance, Iran, Turkey, Iraq)
- Disco

- Dappan koothu
- Doublebugg
- Dougie
- Dragon dance
- Drobushki (Russia)
- Dubotanets (Ukrainian)
- Duranguense
- Dutty Wine - a West Indian, Dancehall-inspired dance

E

- East Coast Swing
- Eisa
- Electro dance
- Electric Slide
- English Country Dance
- Ethnic dance

F

- Fat dance
- Fandango
- Farandole (Provençal)
- Faroese dance
- Farruca

- Flamenco (Spanish/gypsy)
- Folk dance
- Formation dance
- Forró (dance from northeast of Brazil)
- Foxtrot (Ballroom Social)
- The Freddy
- Frug
- Freak dancing
- Funk Brazil

G

- Gaida (Greece)
- Galliard
- Galop
- Garba (folk dance of state of Gujarat, India)
- Gankino (Bulgaria)
- Gavotte (Brittany), Gavot (historical)
- Gigue
- Grinding (dance)
- Grizzly Bear
- Guapacha (dance)
- Gumboot dance (Africa)

- Giddha (Folk dance of Northern India)
- g-slide by Lil Mama

H

- Habanera
- Haka (Māori)
- Hakken (Dutch)
- Halay (Turkish, Folk)
- Hambo (Scandinavian, Folk)
- Hand Dance (Swing, Washington DC and Baltimore MD metropolitan areas, regional)
- Hardcore Dancing (Urban American Hardcore)
- Hasapiko (Greece)* *Headbanging*
- Highland dancing
- Hip hop dance
- Historical dance
- Hitch hike
- Hokey Pokey, also known as Hokey-cokey, Okey-cokey
- Hootchy-Kootchy : Bellydance
- Holubka (Ukrainian, Hutsul, Bukovina, Carpathian Ruthenia)
- Hopak (Ukrainian)
- Hopak-Kolom (Ukrainian)

- House dance
- Hora (many named versions; folk, Bulgarian, Israeli, Romanian, Ukrainian)
- Horan (Crimean Tatars)
- Horon (Turkish, Folk)
- Hornpipe (Ireland)
- Hula
- Hully Gully
- Hustle and its variant, New York Hustle (Club)
    - Latin Hustle
- Humppa (see Music of Finland)
- Hutsulka (Ukrainian, Hutsuls)

I

- Ice dancing
- Ikariotikos (Greece)
- Improv Tribal Style Belly Dance
- Intercessory dance
- International folk dance
- Interpretive dance
- Irish
    - Irish Dance
    - Irish Sean-Nós Dance

- - Irish Stepdance
  - Israeli folk dancing

J

- - Japanese traditional dance (Japanese)
  - Jarabe tapatío
  - Jazz dance
  - Jazz Funk
  - Jenkka (see Music of Finland)
  - Jerkin'
  - Jig Ireland
  - Jig (Scottish country)
  - Jitterbug (Swing)
    - - Cajun Jitterbug
  - Jitterbug Stroll (Line dance, Swing)
  - Jive (Ballroom, International Latin)
  - Joged (Indonesian)
  - John Wall dance
  - Jota (Spanish dance)
  - Jove Malaj Mome (Bulgarian folk dance)
  - Jumpstyle (Techno based dance)

- Jabbawokeez

K

- Kalinka (Russia)
- Kalymnikos (Greece)
- Kamarinskaya (Russia)
- Karsilama (Antikrystos, Marinella) (Greece, Gypsy)
- Karşılama (Serbia, Iran, Turkey)
- Kandian ([sri Lanka])
- Kathak (Classical Indian Dance)
- Kathakali (India, incorporates dance)
- Kazachok (Russia)
- Kerala Natanam (Indian Dance created by Guru Gopinath)
- Khasapiko (Greece)
- Khattak Dance (Pashtun)
- Kizomba (Angola)
- [{Kizomba De Roda - New way to Dance Kizomba}] ({[Angola}])
- Kolo (Slavic)
- Khon (Thai dance)
- Khorovod (Russia)
- Kleistos (Greece)
- Koftos (Greece)

- Kolbasti (Turkey)
- Kolomyjka (Ukrainian)
- Kopanitsa (Bulgaria)
- Kotsari(Armenian: Քոչարի; Turkish: *Koçari*; Greek: Κότσαρι; Georgian: ქოჩარი; Laz: Koçari; Azerbaijani: *Köçəri*)
- Kozachok (Ukrainian)
- Krakowiak (Poland)
- Krishnanattam (India)
- Krumping)
- Kuchipudi (Classical Indian Dance)
- Kuki Lenkhawm Laam (Classical dance form of the Kuki people practised during the times of the Sukte Dynasty)
- Kurdish dance (Iran and Iraq)
- Kujawiak (Poland)
- Kushtdepdi (Turkmen)

L

- La Jota
- LambadaKochari(Armenian folk dance)
- Lambeth Walk
- Lancer (Quadrille)
- Landler (Quadrille)
- Lap dance

- Latin dance
- Lavani
- Lavolta
- Ländler (Austria)
- Lerikos (Greece)
- LeRoc (Modern Jive, Ceroc)
- Letkajenkka (also known as Letkis, Letkajenka, Letkiss, Letka-Enka, Let's Kiss Jenka, La Yenka)
- Leventikos (Greece)
- Limbo (dancers pass under horizontal pole)
- Lindy Hop (Swing)
- Line dance
- Lion dance
- Liscio (Italian traditional music and dance inspired to Waltz, Polka and Mazurka)
- Locking
- Long Sword
- Loure (historical)
- Lyrical hip hop dance
- Lyrical jazz dance
- Lyrical contempery

M

- Macarena
- Madison (Line dance)
- Maglalatik (Folk Dance of Philippines)
- Malaguena
- Mambo (American Ballroom, of Cuban origin)
- Mandra (Mandilatos) (Balkan)
- Maneo (Galicia)
- Manila Swing
- Manipuri (Classical Indian Dance form)
- Mapale
- Marinera
- Marinella (Greece)
- Mashed Potato
- Matachin (Matachines)
- Maypole dance
- Maxixe (Social)
- Mazur (dance) (Poland)
- Mazurka (Poland)

- Medieval dance
- Melbourne Shuffle (Australia)
- Merengue (Latin Club)
- Metelytsia ((Ukrainian), khorovod)
- Milonga (see Argentine Tango)
- Minuet
- Modern dance
- Modern contemporary
- Modern Jive
- Molly dance
- Mohiniattam
- Monkey
- Moonwalker
- Morris dance
- Moshing
- Muiñeira (Galicia)
    - Carballesa
    - Chouteira
    - Contrapaso
    - Golpe
    - Muiñeira ribeirana

- Muiñeira vella
- Pandeirada
- Piruxada
- Redonda
- Regueifa
- Walk it out

N

- Novelty and fad dances
- The Nutbush
- Nama Stap (Namibia)

O

- Oberek (also called *Obertas* or *Ober*, Poland)
- Odissi AKA orissi (Orissa, India)
- Onei
- Over/Under

P

- Pachanga
- Palo de Mayo (Nicaragua), *Afro-Caribbean influence, not to be confused with* Maypole dance
- Pagode

- Pangalatok (Philippines)
- Pantsula (South Africa)
- Parasol dance (Japan)
- Partner dance
- Participation dance
- Para Para
- Passacaglia (Passacaille) (historical)
- Passepied (historical)
- Pasillo
- Paso Doble (Ballroom, International Latin)
- Pavane (historical)
- Peabody (ballroom)
- Peewee style (originated by Pee-wee Herman in Pee-wee's Big Adventure)
- Pentozalis (Greece)
- Persian dance (Iran).
- Pidikhtos (Greece)
    - Kastrinos Pidikhtos (Greece)
    - Malevyziotiko Pidikhtos (Greece)
- Pendozalis (Greece)
- Pole dancing
- Pop, Lock, and Drop It (Hip hop)

- Pogo (A punk dance, consisting of jumping up and down)
- Pogonisios (Greece)
- Polka - many named versions (Ballroom, Folk, Historical)
- Polka-mazurka
- Polonaise
- Pony
- Pols (Norway, Folk, see Polska)
- Pom Squad
- Polska (pl.: Polskor; Sweden, Folk)
- Prophetic dance
- Pryvit (Ukrainian)
- Pyrrhichios (Dance from Pontos; Greek Black Sea)
- Push (Swing, Texas)

Q

- Qasemabadi (a northern Persian style)
- Quadrille
- Quickstep (Ballroom)
- Quebradita (Mexico)
- FINE (United States of America)

R

- Raas
- Rain dancing
- Ramvong (Cambodia)
- Rapper sword
- Raqs Sharqi ("belly dance")
- Rebetiko dances (Greece)
- Redowa
- Reel (Irish and Scottish)
- Regency dance
- Reggae
- Reggaeton
- Renaissance dance
- Rigaudon, Rigadoon
- River Dancing
- Robot dance
- Rock and Roll
    - Acrobatic Rock'n'Roll
- Round dance (two kinds: circular chain, couples)

- Rumba (Ballroom: International Latin & American Rhythm, Folk)
  - Cuban Rumba (Ballroom dance as of the beginning of the century, e.g., "The Peanut Vendor" piece)

S

- Salsa (Latin Club)
- Salsa Rueda (Latin Club, Round)
- Saltatio (Roman)
- Sambalpuri (India)
- Samba
  - Samba dance
  - Samba de Gafieira
  - Samba (ballroom)
- Sarabande (Saraband)
- Sardana (Catalonia)
- Sattriya dance
- Saunter
- Schottische
- Scottish country dance
- Scottish highland dance

- Schoolcraft
- Sean-Nós Dance (Ireland - Irish Dance in Sean Nós "Old Style")
- Seguidilla (Spanish, folk)
- Sequence dance
- Serra (Greece)
- Set Dance Ireland
- Sevillana (Spain)
- Shag (Swing)
    - Carolina Shag
    - Collegiate Shag
    - St. Louis Shag
- Shake
- Shim Sham (Line dance)
- Shimmy
- Shuffle
- Siganos (Greece)
- Single Swing (Single Time Swing)
- Sirtaki (Syrtaki, Zorba) (Greece)
- Skank (dance)
- Skip jive
- Slängpolska (Sweden, Folk, see Polska)

- Slip jig (Ireland)
- Slosh (Scotland)
- Slow dance
- Slow Foxtrot - also known as Foxtrot and Slowfox (Ballroom)
- Social dance
- Son (Mayan, Guatemala/Mexico)
- Sousta (Greece)
    - Bulgarian Sousta (Greece)
    - Cretan Sousta (Greece)
    - Dodecanese Sousta (Greece)
    - Macedonian Sousta (Greece)
    - Megarian Sousta (Greece)
- The Spongebob
- Square dance
    - Traditional square dance
    - Modern Western square dance
- Stage diving
- (Do The) Standing Still (The Table, 1977)
- Stanky Legg (GS Boys)
- Step dance Ireland
- Street dance

- Swim
- Swing (both as family of dances and as specific Texas dance)
- Swing Jive (Modern Jive, Club)
- Swing Roc (Modern Jive, Club)
- Suzie Q
- Syrtos (Greece)
    - Cretan Syrtos (Greece)
    - Kalamatianos Syrtos (Mainland Syrtos) (Greece)
    - Kapoutzidon Syrtos (Greece)
    - Nisiotiko Syrtos (Island Syrtos) (Greece)
    - Silyvriano Syrtos (Greece)

T

- Tambourin (Provençal)
- Tango (Ballroom, Social, Club)
    - Argentine Tango - also known as Tango Argentino (Social)
    - Uruguayan Tango - also known as Tango Uruguayo (Social)
    - Ballroom Tango - competitive and social dance styles
    - Brazilian Tango - see Maxixe
    - Finnish tango
    - Chinese tango
- Tanoura (Egyptian dance)

- Tap Charleston (see Lindy Hop)
- Tap dance
- Tarantella (Italian, folk)
- Tau'olunga (Tongan or Samoan - Polynesian origins)
- Tecktonik ("tck")
- Texas Tommy (see Lindy Hop)
- Thizz Dance
- Tik (Greece)
- Tinikling (Philippines)
- Time Warp
- Tourdion (historical)
- Traditional dance
- Tranky Doo (Swing, Line dance)
- Trata (Greece)
- Trepak (Russian, folk)
- Tribal Style Belly Dance
- Troika (Folk, Russian, Cajun)
- Tropotianka (Ukrainian, Rusyn, Carpathian Ruthenia, Bukovina, Hutsuls)
- Troubadou (Haiti)
- Tsakonikos (Greece)

- Tsamiko (Greece)
- Tsifteteli (Tsifte-Teli) (Çifte-telli) (Turkish) (Greece)(Gypsy)(Arabic)
- Tsirigotikos (Kythiraikos, Bourdaris) (Greece)
- Tsyganochka, ("Gypsie Girl") Russian
- Turf Dancing
- Tumba
- Twist
- Two-step
  - Cajun Two Step
  - Country/Western Two-step
  - Nightclub two-step - also known as California Two-step, abbrn: NC2S
- Theatre jazz
  - Progressive Double Two

U

- Universal Peace, Dances of
- Ukrainian dance
- Upa or Upa Habanera, claimed by some to be the origin of merengue music and dance.
- Uvyvanets (Ukrainian, Carpathian Ruthenia, Rusyns, Lemkos, Hutsuls)
- Pole Dancing

V
- Valeta (a dance to waltz music)
- Vals (Argentina, tango style)
    - Valse à deux temps (Valse à deux pas)
- Verbunkos
- Vesnianka (Ukrainian, a type of khorovod)
- Vintage dance
- Vogue (dance)
- Volte (also Volta, La volta, or Lavolta, Renaissance)

W
- Waltz (ballroom, social)
    - Boston (dance)
        - Walking Boston
    - Cajun Waltz
    - Dream Waltz
    - Elizabeth Waltz
    - Cross-step Waltz (Cross Step Waltz)
    - Five-step Waltz (Five Step Waltz)
    - Hesitation Waltz
    - Slow waltz - known as *Waltz* in ballroom context (ballroom)
    - Viennese Waltz (ballroom, social)

- - Valse à deux temps (Valse à deux pas)
- Watusi (fad dance)
- West Coast Swing ("WCS"; Swing, United States)
- Western swing (United States)
  - Classic WCS
  - Funky chick
  - Sophisticated Swing (an older name of WCS)
- Western promenade dance
- Whip (Swing, Texas)
- Winterguard
- Wolosso (Ivory Coast)
- Worship dance

X

- Xibelani (traditional Shangaan (South Africa))

Y

- Yablochko (Russian, folk)
- Yerakina (Greece)
- YMCA
- Yakshagana (India, Karnataka)
- Yowla (rifle dance from (UAE)

Z

- Zapateado (Spain)
- Zeibekiko (also spelled Zeibetiko, Zembetiko, Zebetiko, and Zembekiko; Greece)
- Zeibeks (Turkey)
- Zonaradiko (Thrace)
- Zorba's dance (of Greek origin)
- Zouk (Brazil, Haiti, Guadeloupe, Martinique)
- Zouk-Lambada (Brazil)
- Zumba (Colombia)
- Zydeco (Louisiana, U.S.)

www.ingramcontent.com/pod-product-compliance
Lightning Source LLC
Chambersburg PA
CBHW032113090426
42743CB00007B/335